Dog Shaming

Dog Shaming

PASCALE LEMIRE

 THREE RIVERS PRESS • NEW YORK

Library of Congress Cataloging-in-Publication Data
Lemire, Pascale.
Dog shaming / Pascale Lemire.
pages   cm
1. Dogs—Pictorial works. 2. Dogs—Humor. 3. Photography of dogs. I. Title.
SF430.L45 2013   636.7—dc23   2013023473

ISBN 978-0-385-34934-5
eISBN 978-0-385-34935-2

Printed in the United States of America

Book design by Maria Elias and Jaclyn Reyes
Cover design by Nupoor Gordon
Cover photograph: © Jordan Curtis-Sherrod (Sugar's mom)

2   4   6   8   10   9   7   5   3   1

First Edition

I would like to dedicate this book to my wonderful husband, Mike. None of this would have been possible without his support, love, and computer knowledge! I'd also like to dedicate this book to our two rescue wiener dogs, Beau and Dasha, because without them, there'd be no *Dog Shaming*.

Introduction

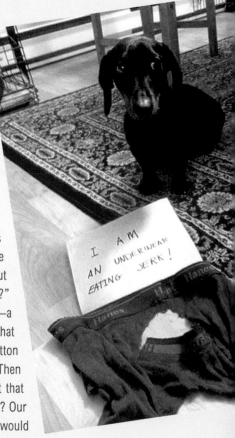

Dog Shaming.

A term almost unheard of a year ago. Today it has become a household name among dog lovers everywhere. It all started in August 2012, when my dog ate my fiancé Mike's underwear. We were sitting in bed one night, reading from our respective tablets, when we heard one of our two dogs chewing . . . something. "Who's under the bed? What are they chewing?!?!" Mike yelled. He reached down and pulled Beau, our male wiener dog, out from under the bed frame. "What are you eating, buddy?" he asked. By the time Mike saw what Beau was chewing—a pair of Mike's boxer-briefs—they had been destroyed. All that was left was the elastic band and shredded pieces of cotton fabric. We sat in bed staring at each other, incredulous. Then almost simultaneously, we burst out laughing. How was it that this fifteen-pound dog could have ingested so much fabric? Our laughter turned to concern when we realized that Beau would eventually have to pass all that fabric! (And guess who would be cleaning it up?)

In a stroke of genius, Mike wrote up a sign that read "I am an underwear-eating jerk!" and put it next to Beau and the chewed-up underwear. I had always blogged about how destructive and troublesome our little Beau was, but I'd never had photographic evidence— now we had proof. Beau hung his head in shame as if he knew why he was being scolded. Mike snapped a photo, which I then posted to my blog. With that, *Dog Shaming* was born.

Within twenty-four hours, my blog post had received almost a thousand comments. (I was worried Mike would be upset that his underwear had been viewed in a public forum by a thousand people, but he remained unfazed.) The funny thing is, other dog owners wanted in on it, and people started sending in their own dogs' shames, which I dutifully posted. I could barely keep up! Soon the media—CNN, *People* magazine, and MSNBC— came calling. All I could do was squeal and shout, "Mike! Mike! Your underwear is on TV again!" The blog had become a bona fide phenomenon. I was deluged with submissions, and taking care of the blog quickly became a full-time job.

Barfing, chasing, chewing, biting, farting, stealing, jumping, running away, human-humping—I was astonished by the range of dog indiscretions. How can creatures so cute be capable of such outrageous behavior and downright grossness? Consider the category of eating-what-they-shouldn't. People have sent in photos of their dogs who had eaten:

socks

underwear

a pound of butter

a cup of sugar (including the plastic container the sugar was in)

walls and baseboards

laptops, cell phones, and tablets

freshly cut Valentine's Day flowers

chocolate (too many times to count)

garbage (too many times to count)

soap

dog training books

an octopus (!)

What you'll find in this book are never-before-seen photos from the vault here at *Dog Shaming* headquarters—with a handful of classics. You might even recognize your own dog in some of these shots in a "My dog does that! And that! And definitely that!" kind of way. Although the main goal of Dog Shaming is to poke fun at our most favorite furry creatures, it also shows pet owners that they're not the only ones to have a mischievous animal. Every dog is just one hand-lettered sign away from the perfect *Dog Shaming* picture, after all! We all know our dogs misbehave; there are no perfect dogs. Anyone who tells you, "Oh you'll never see my dog on that website; she's perfect," is either lying to you or is still blaming the dryer for all his missing socks.

I have often wondered how *Dog Shaming* got so big, so quickly. Internet memes are such a mystery to me. They're nonexistent one day and everywhere the next. I think when it came to *Dog Shaming*, it was as if people were just waiting for an outlet to vent their frustrations about their dogs' inexplicable behavior in a fun way. Submitting a photo and getting like-minded dog lovers (millions of them!) to laugh with you is cathartic. Sure, we're "shaming" our dogs, but it's with the most possible affection, as we're replacing the screen door they broke, taking them for X-rays because they ate an engagement ring, or apologizing to the clerk at the pet store for the puddle of vomit near the treat bar. We give them unconditional love, and they give it right back. The shaming is done with love.

Of course, it doesn't hurt that dogs can't read.

Woof.

Pascale Lemire,
CEO OF *DOG SHAMING*

rg

YUM

The

tear

hew

FRIENDS

uilty

Love

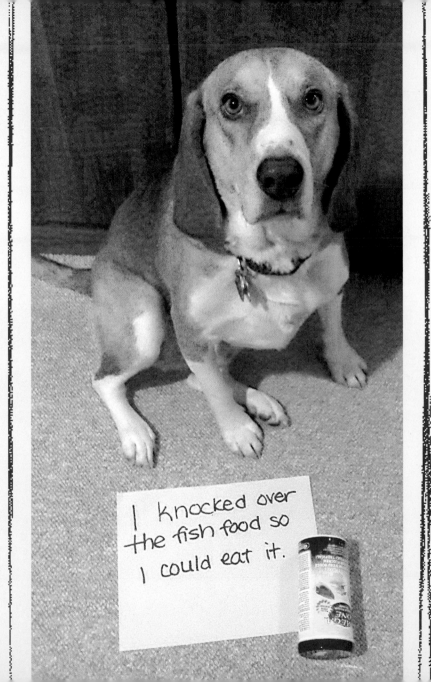

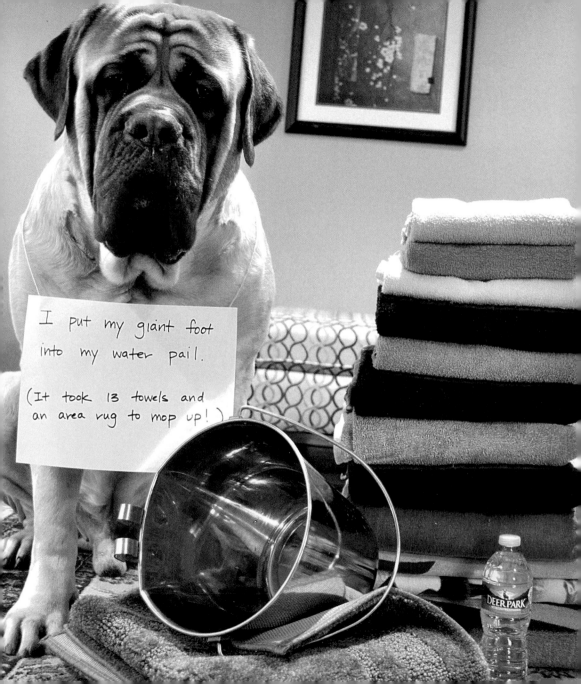

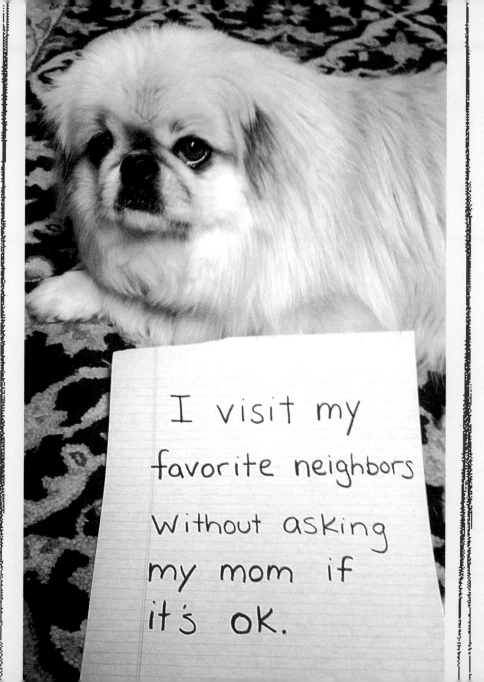

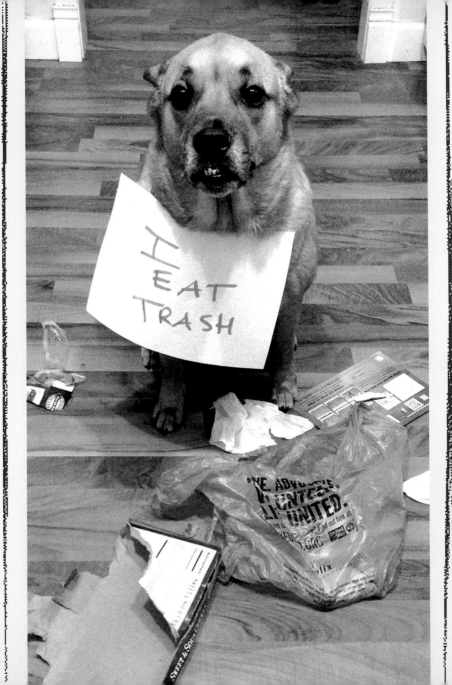

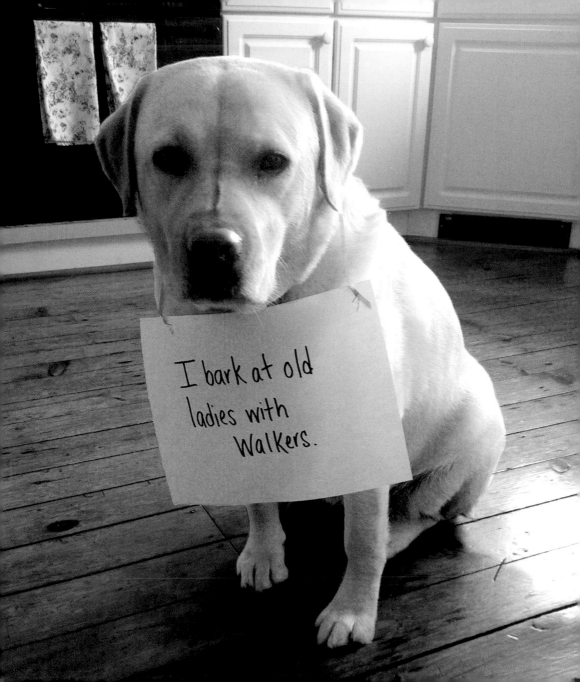

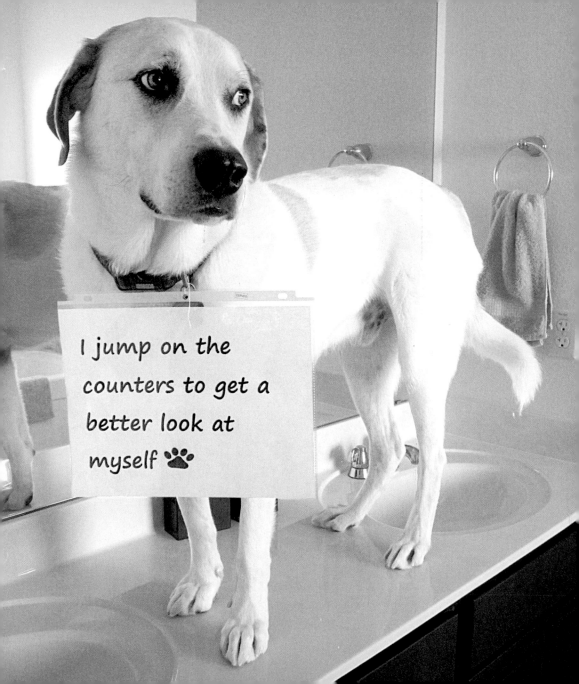

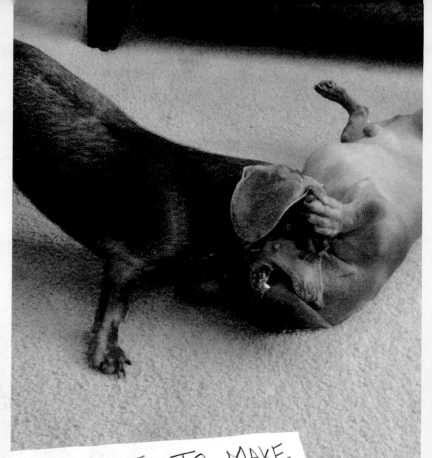

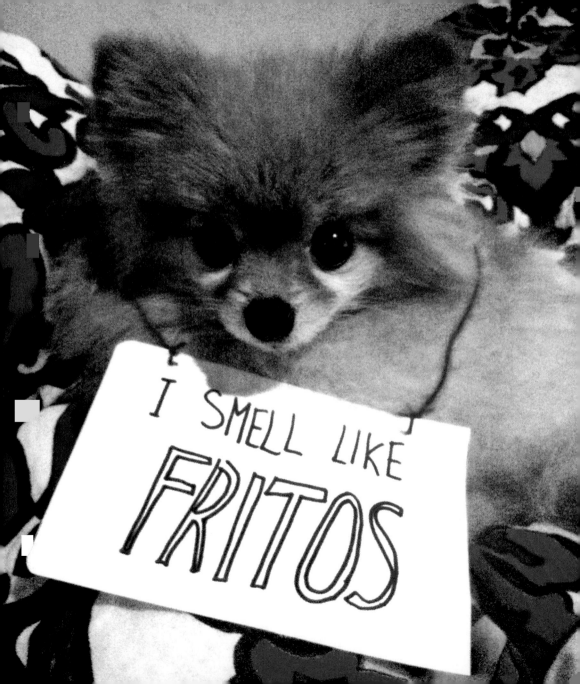

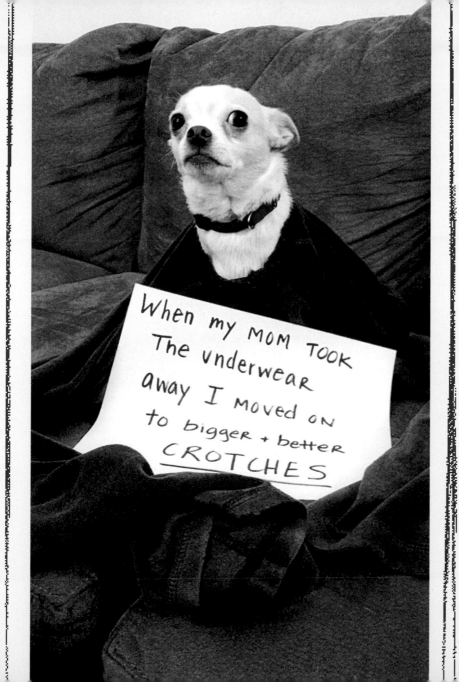

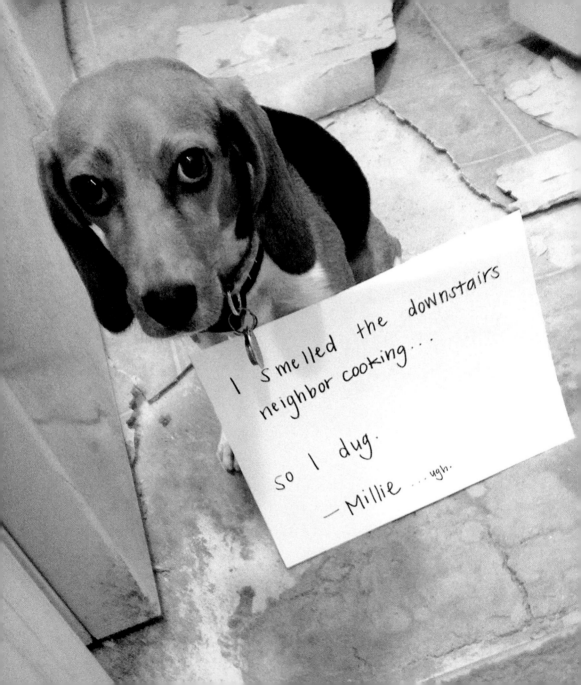

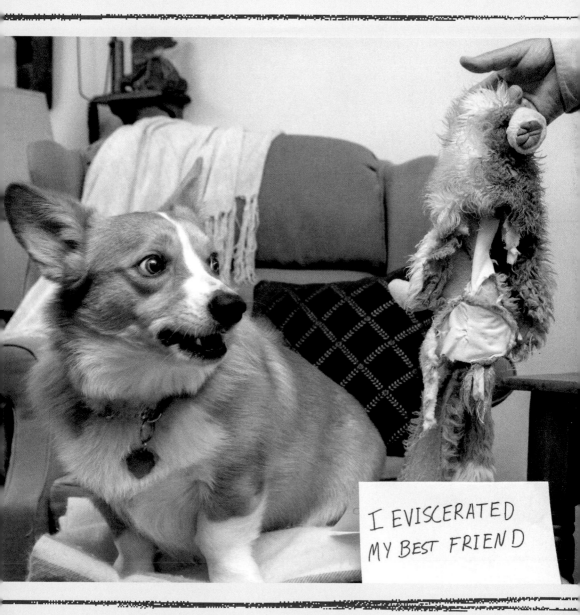

I EVISCERATED MY BEST FRIEND

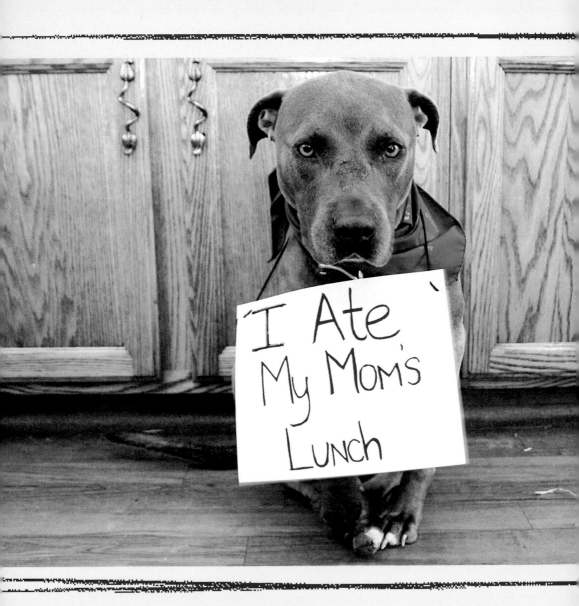

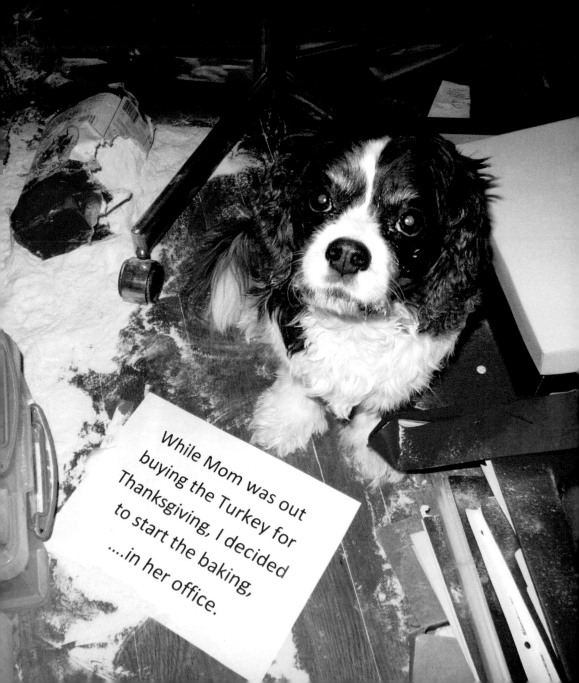

While Mom was out buying the Turkey for Thanksgiving, I decided to start the baking, ...in her office.

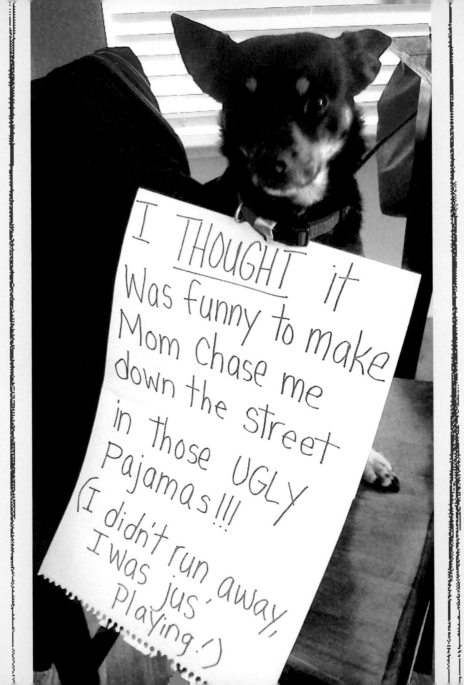

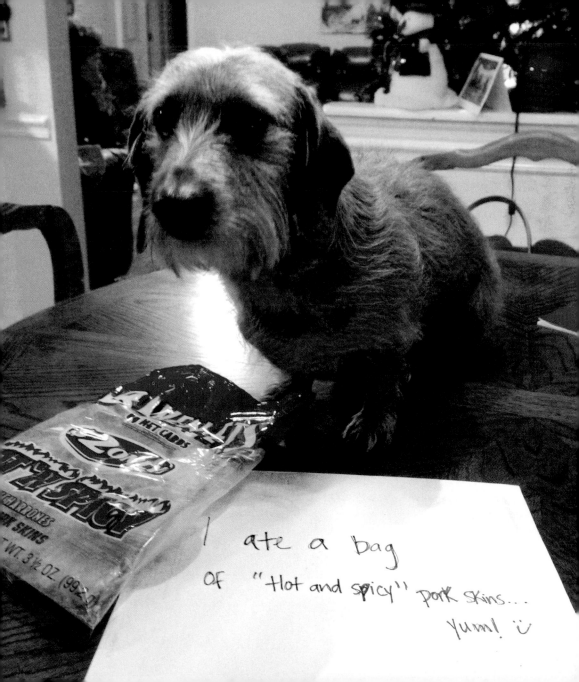

I ate a bag
of "Hot and spicy" pork skins...
Yum! :)

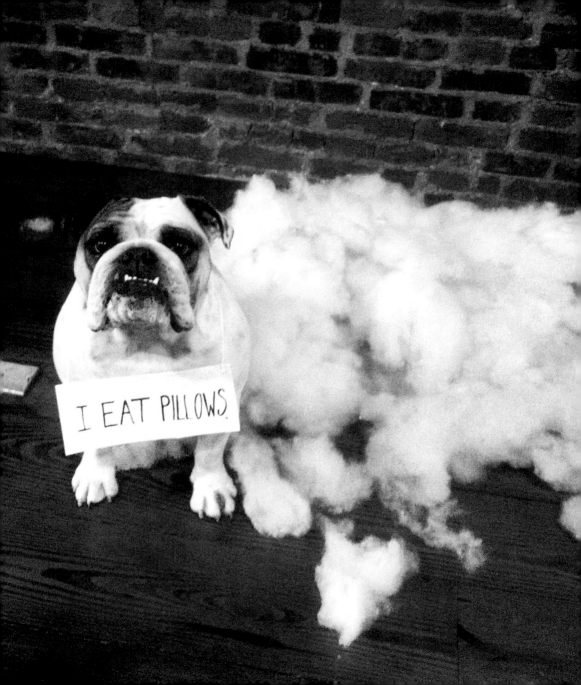

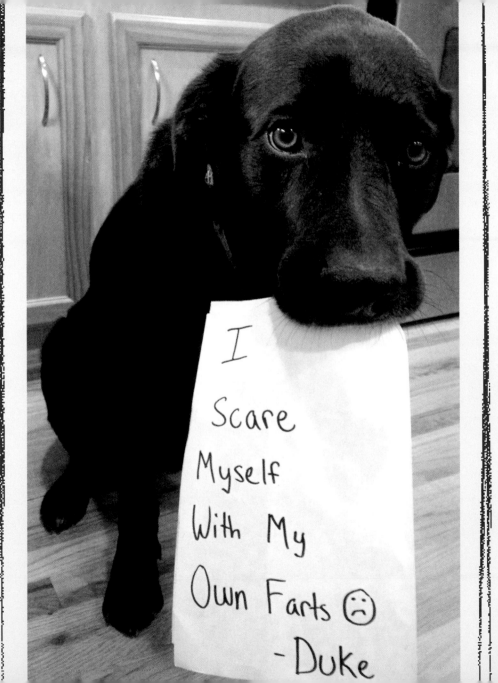

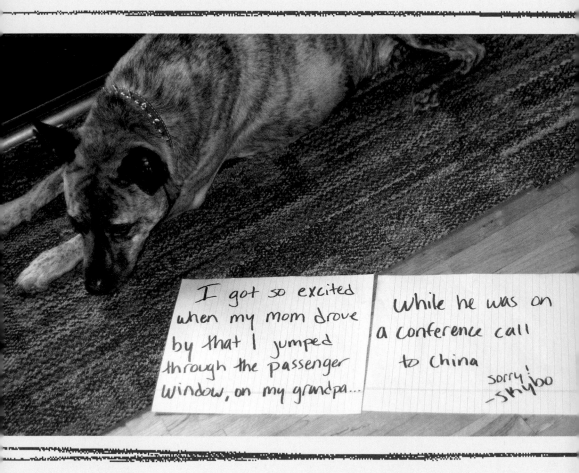

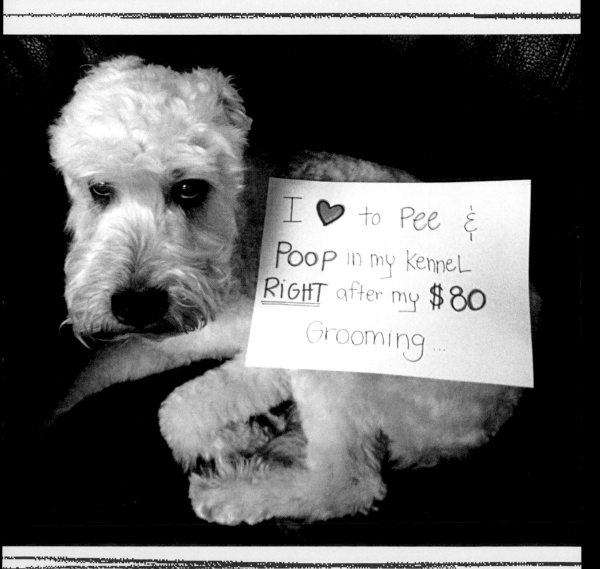

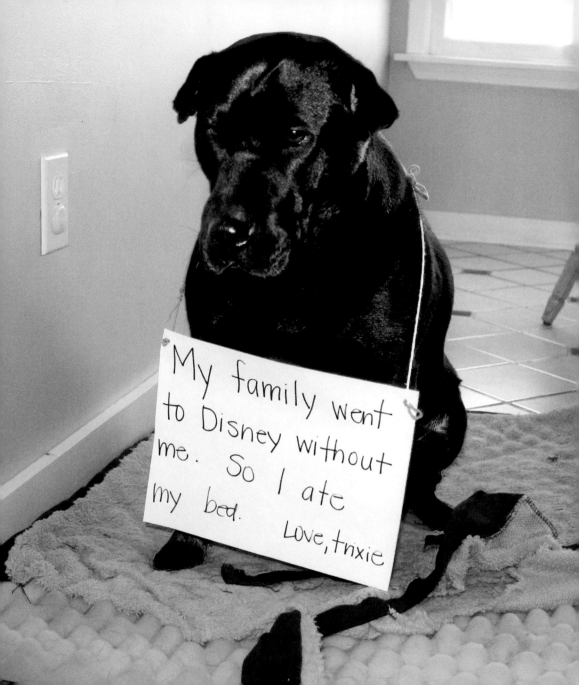

My family went to Disney without me. So I ate my bed. Love, trixie

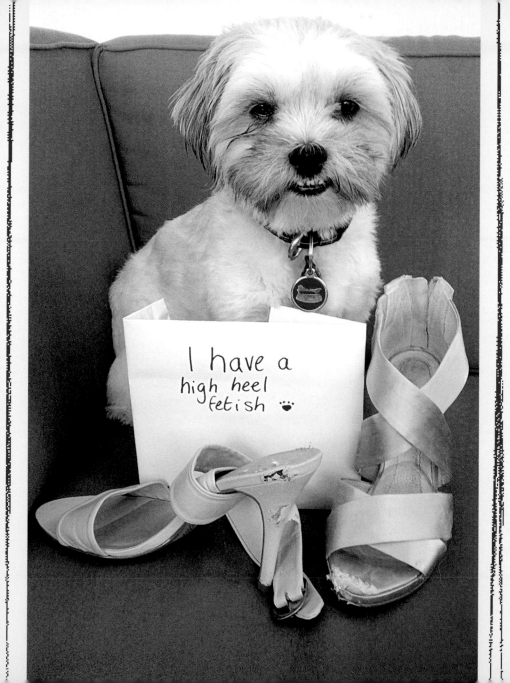

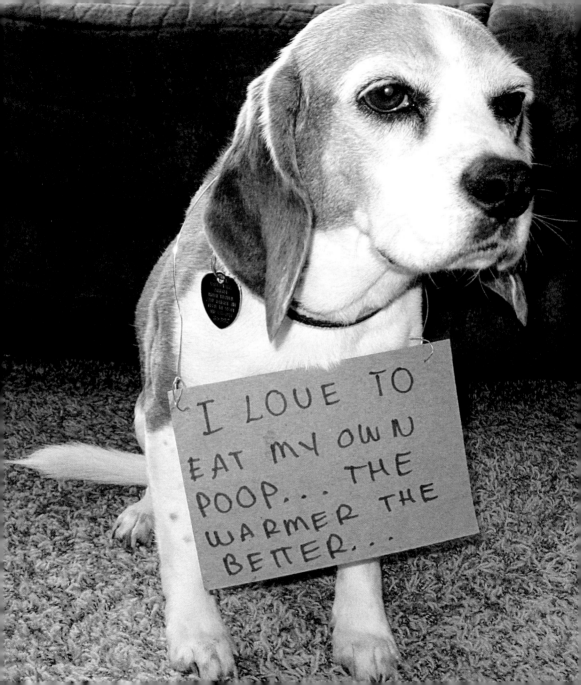

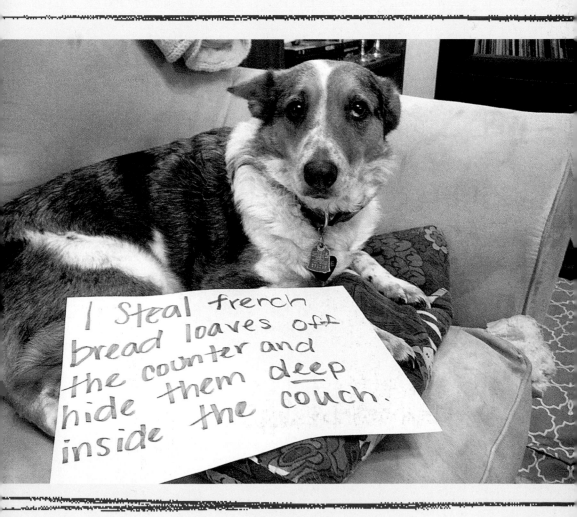

I steal french bread loaves off the counter and hide them deep inside the couch.

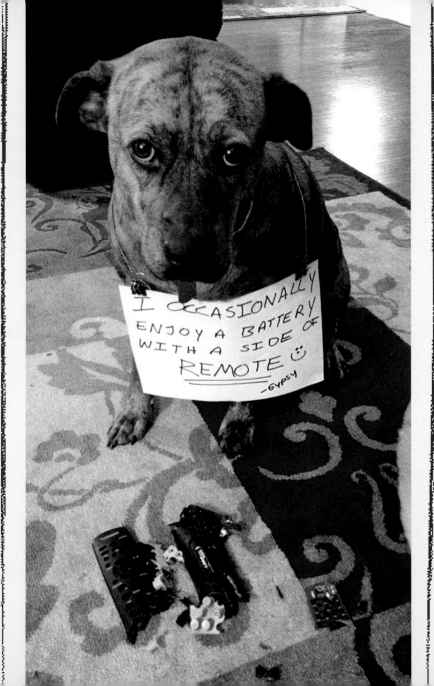

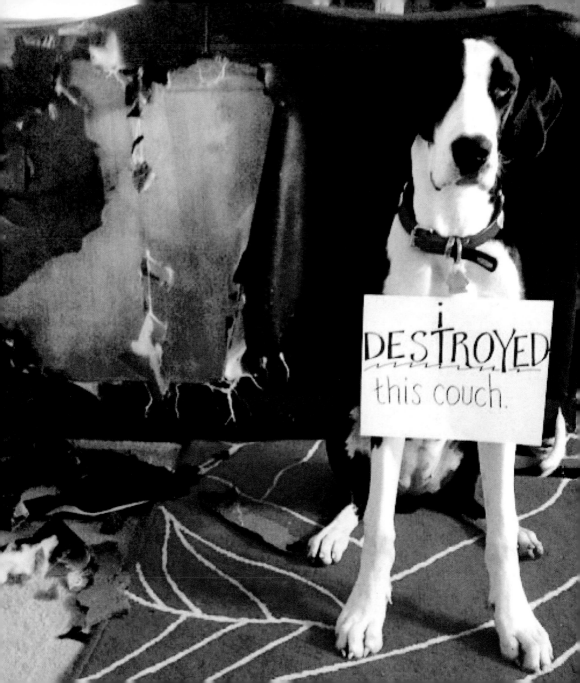

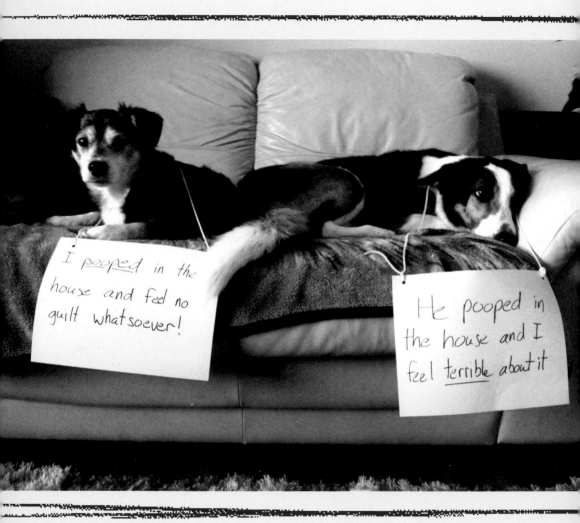

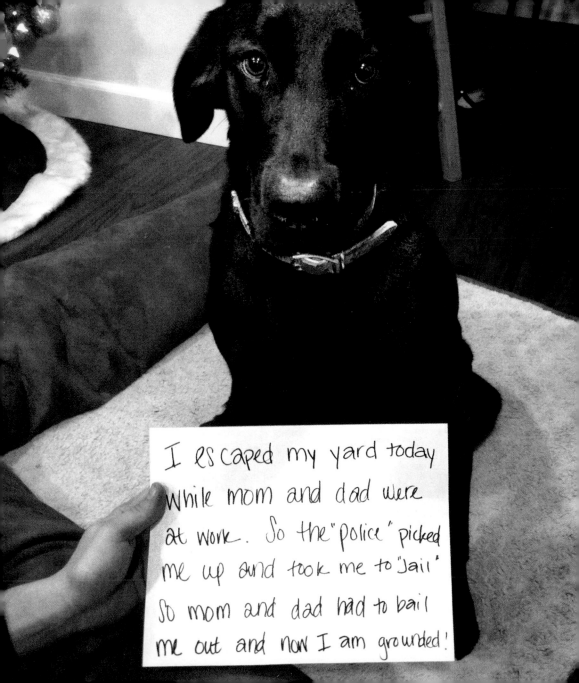

I escaped my yard today while mom and dad were at work. So the "police" picked me up and took me to "jail". So mom and dad had to bail me out and now I am grounded!

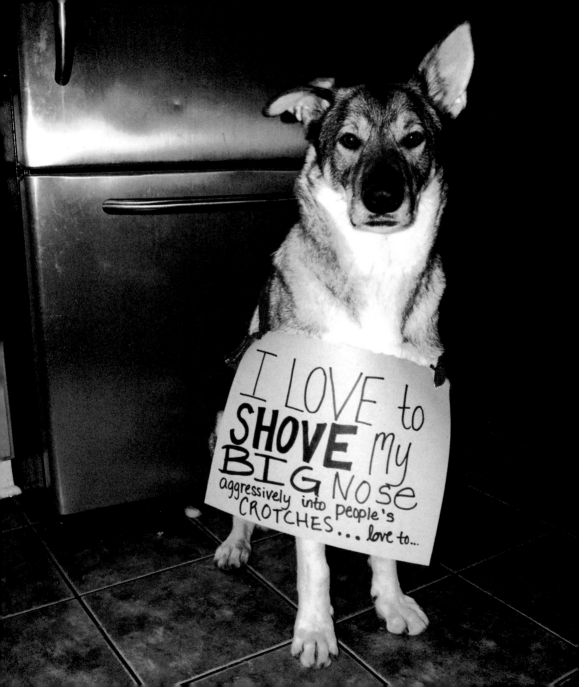

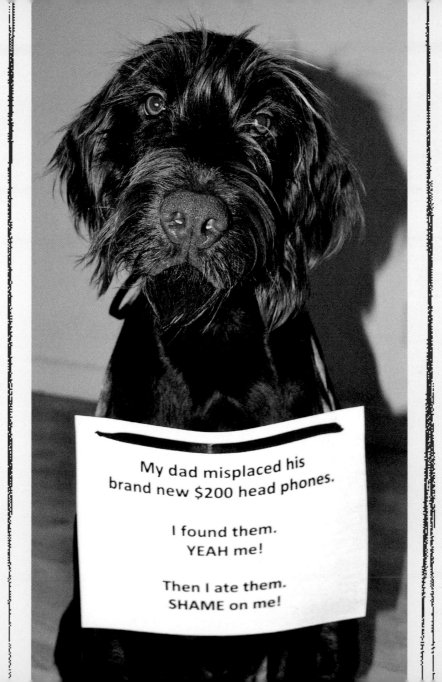

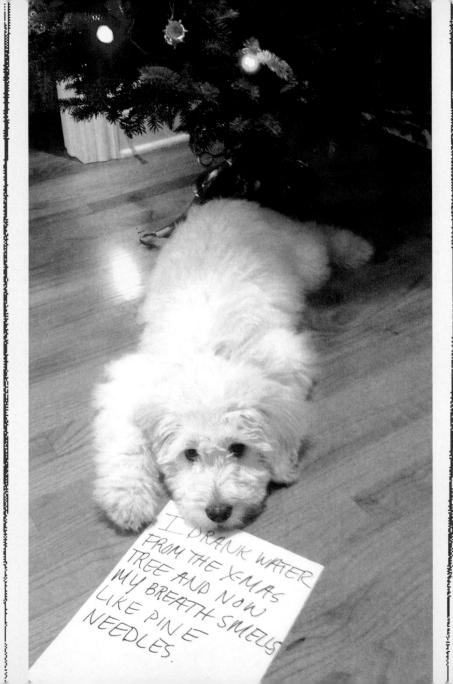

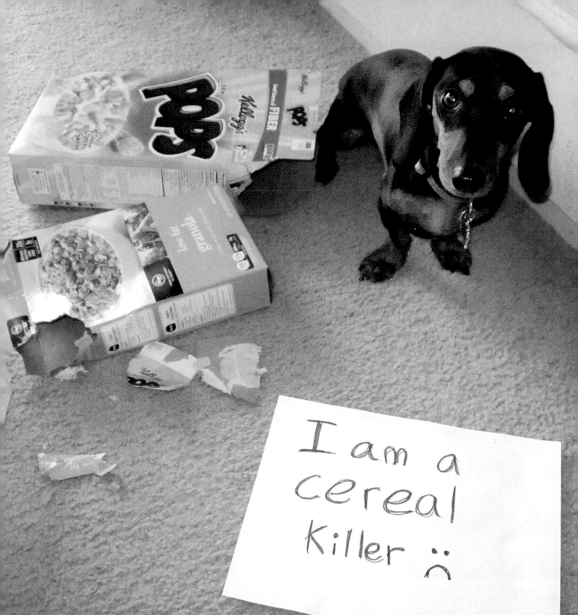

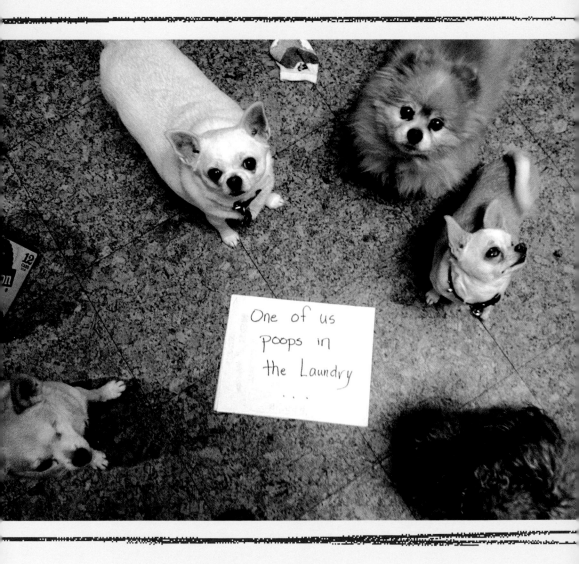

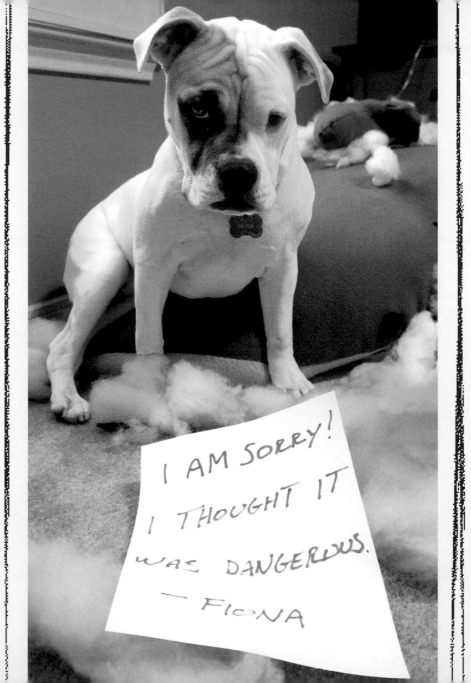

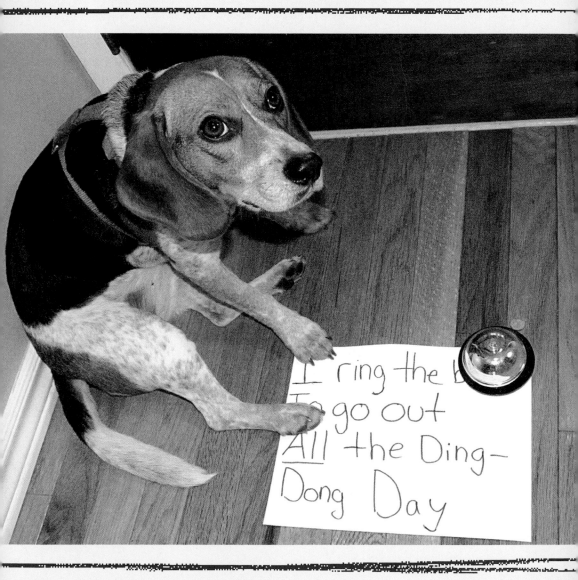

I ring the b[ell]
To go out
All the Ding-
Dong Day

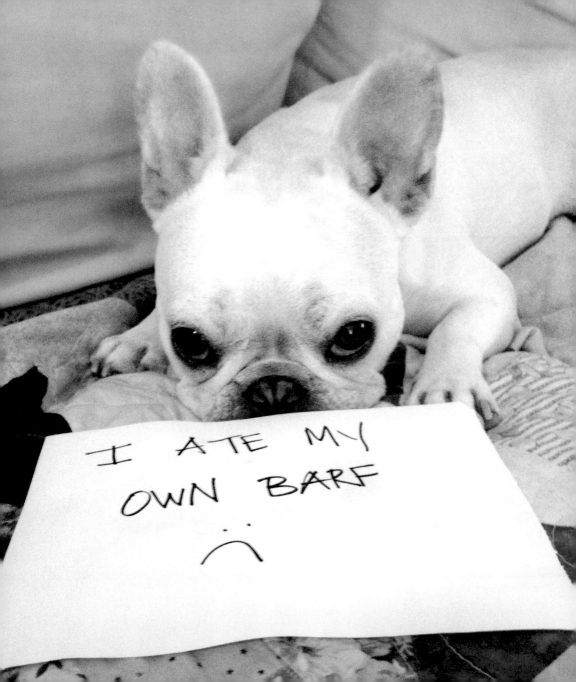

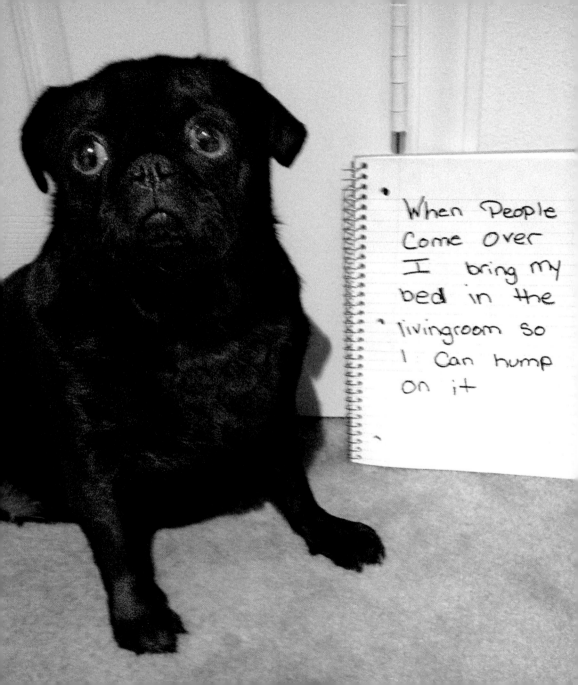

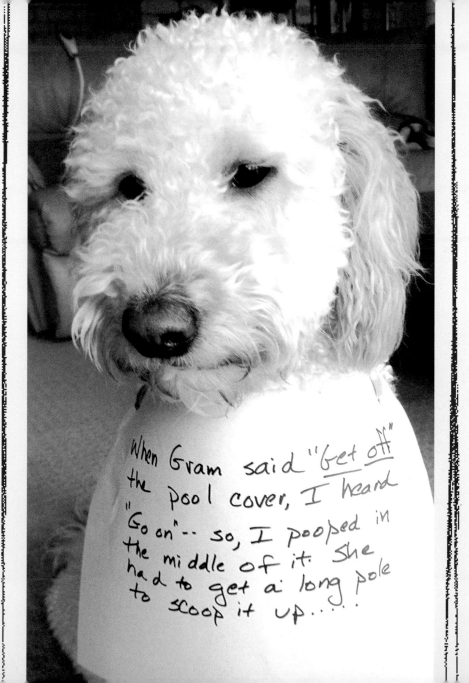

When Gram said "<u>Get off</u>" the pool cover, I heard "Go on"-- so, I pooped in the middle of it. She had to get a long pole to scoop it up....!

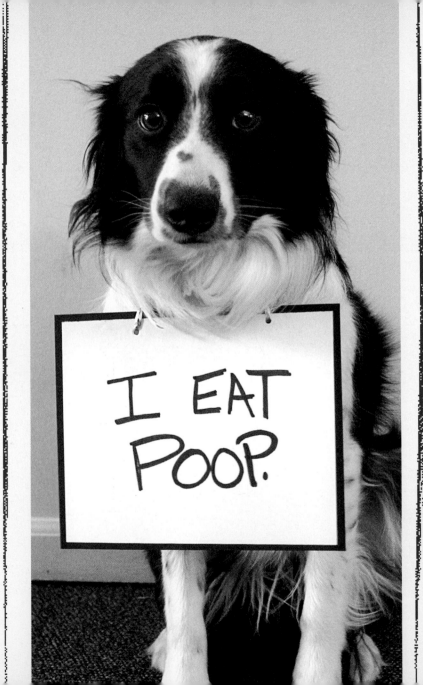

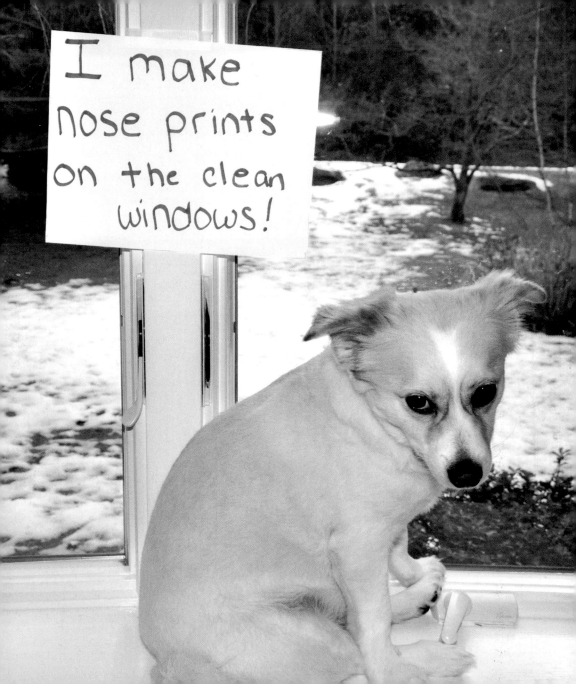

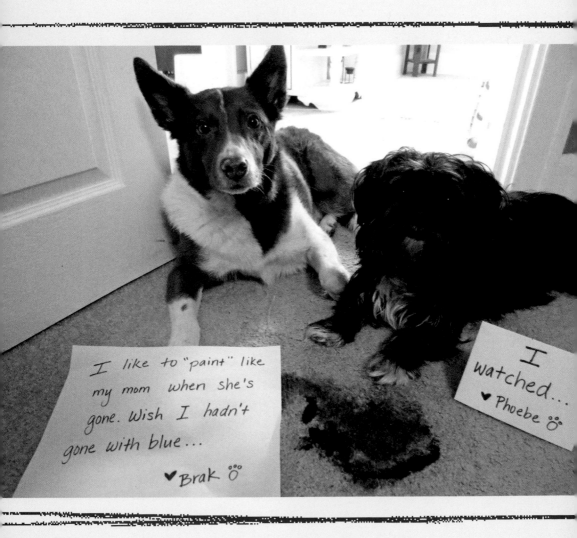

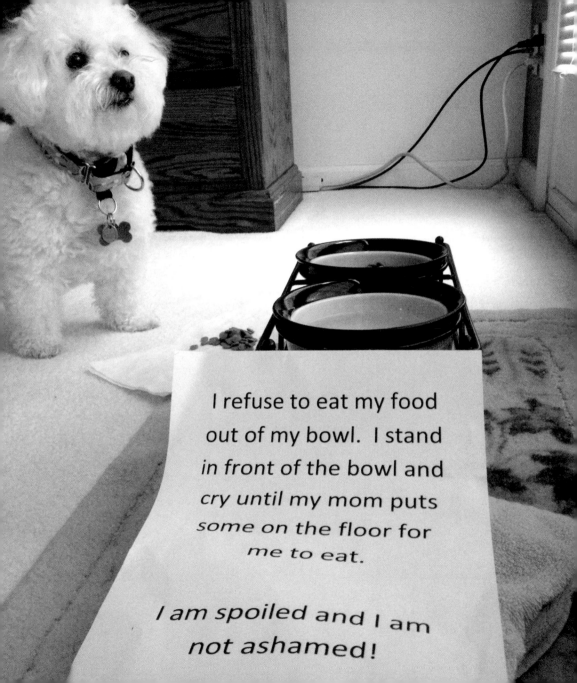

I refuse to eat my food out of my bowl. I stand in front of the bowl and *cry* until my mom puts *some* on the floor for me to eat.

I am spoiled and *I am not ashamed!*

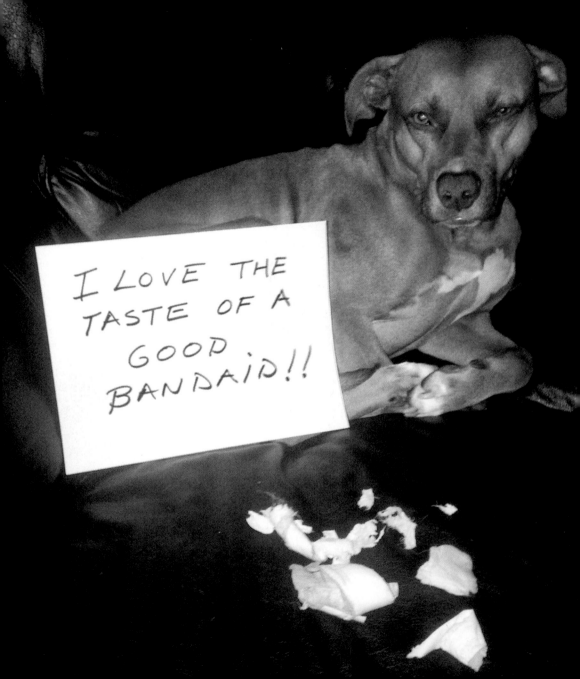

I like to give my mommy kisses after licking my butt.

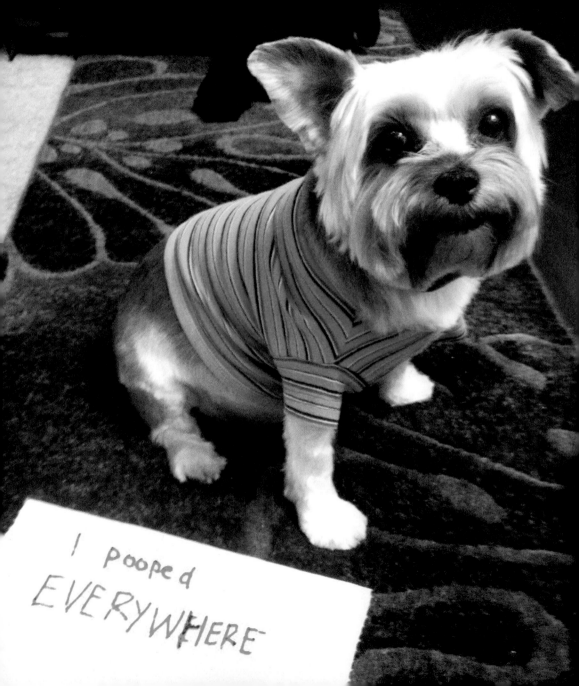

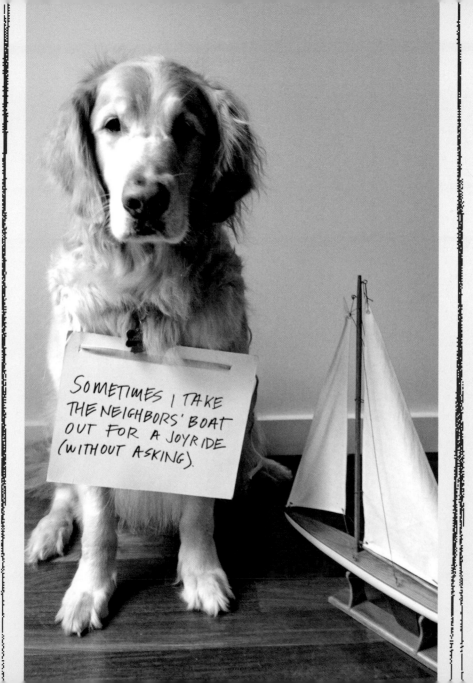

SOMETIMES I TAKE THE NEIGHBORS' BOAT OUT FOR A JOYRIDE (WITHOUT ASKING).

Hello.
My name is Lily
I'm a dishwasher
licking a-holic...

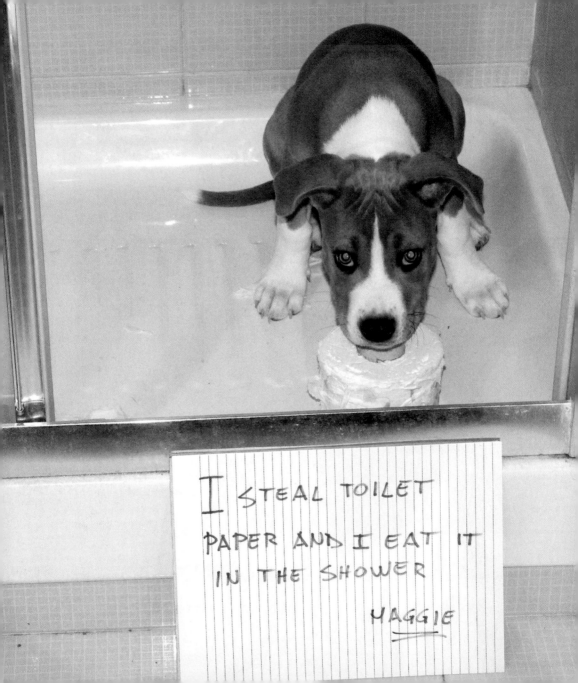

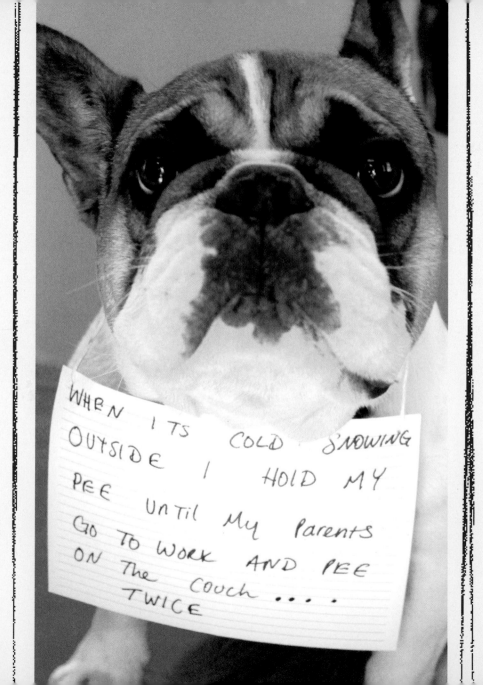

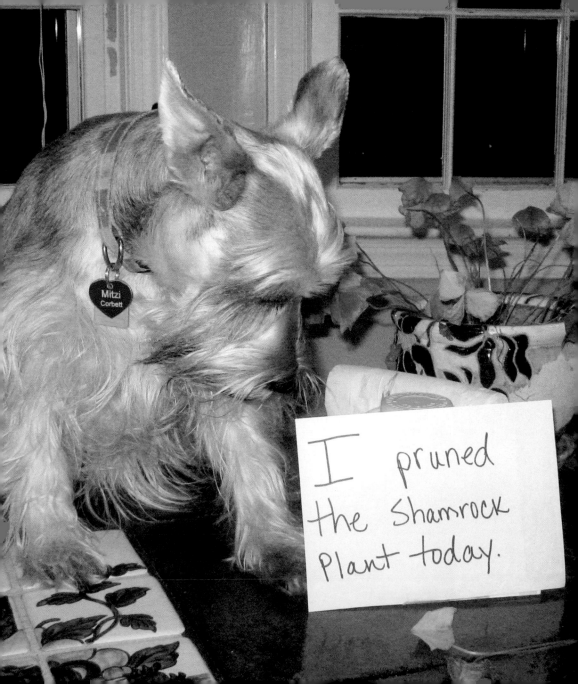

I'm in the Box of Shame Today b/c I like to eat everything I see!

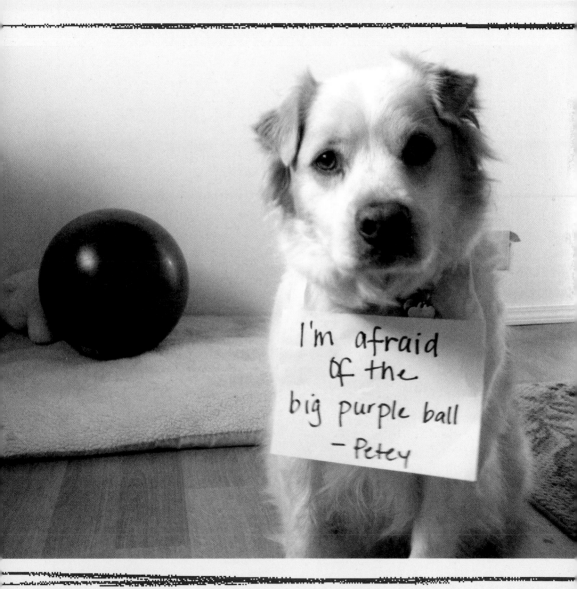

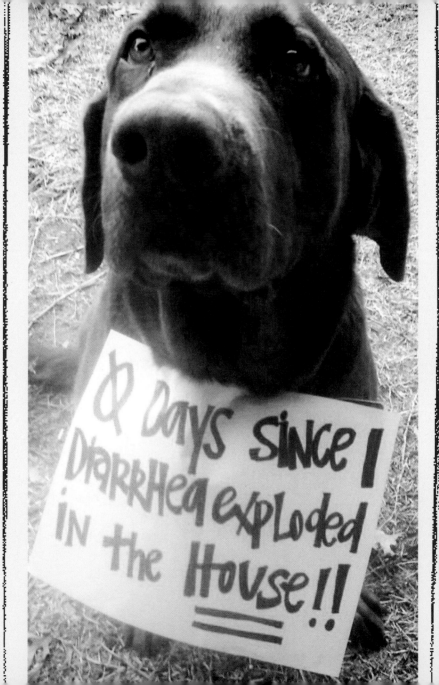

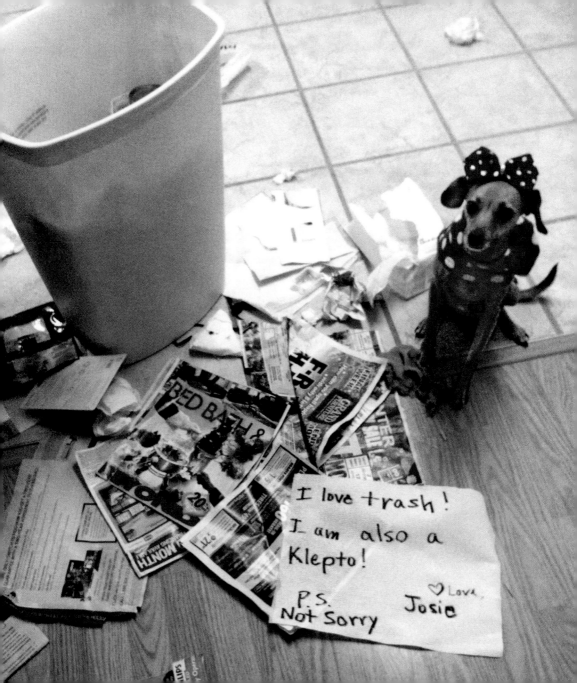

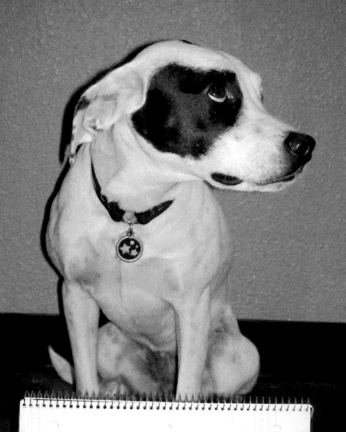

I WAKE MY PEOPLE UP
EVERY NIGHT BARKING AT
PEOPLE OUTSIDE, BUT
SLEEP THROUGH THE
ROBBER IN THE NEXT
ROOM OVER

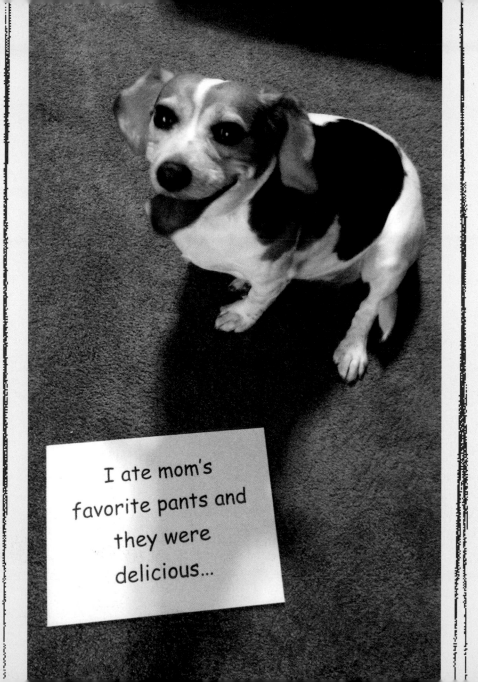

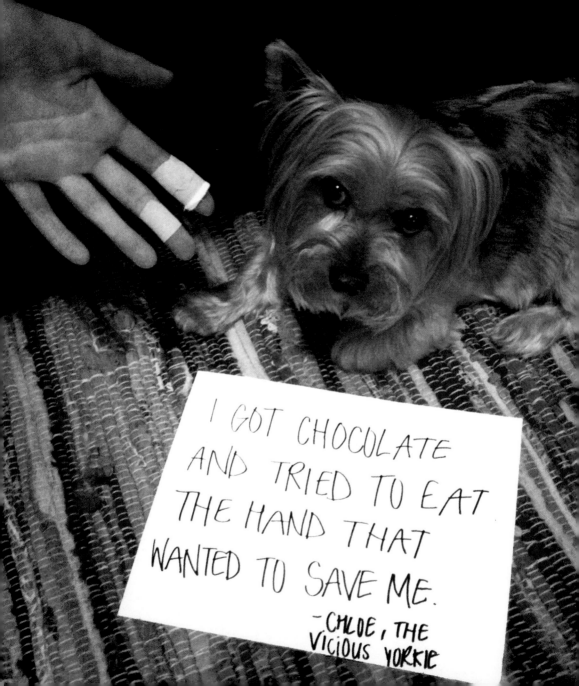

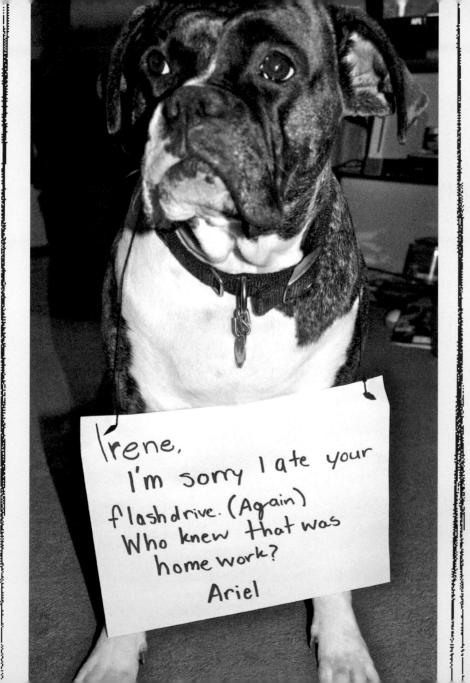

Irene,
I'm sorry I ate your
flashdrive. (Again)
Who knew that was
homework?
Ariel

I dropped my dirty kong in the toilet.
You gonna get it for me?

-Dee Dee

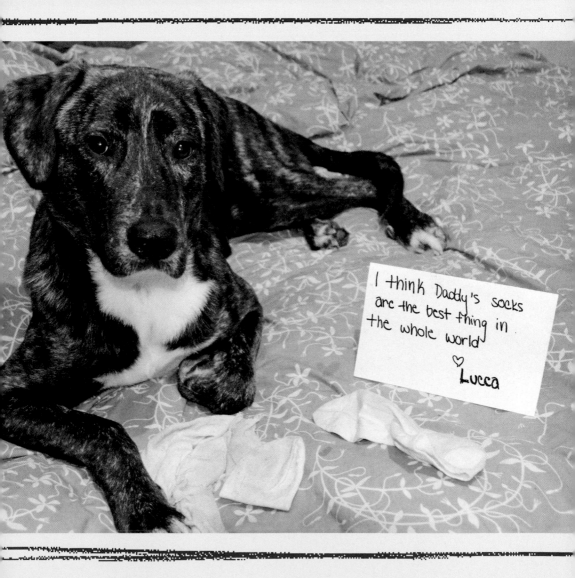

I think Daddy's socks are the best thing in the whole world ♡ Lucca

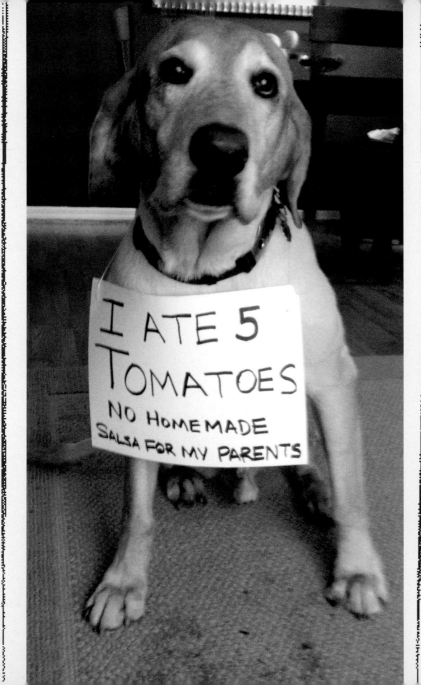

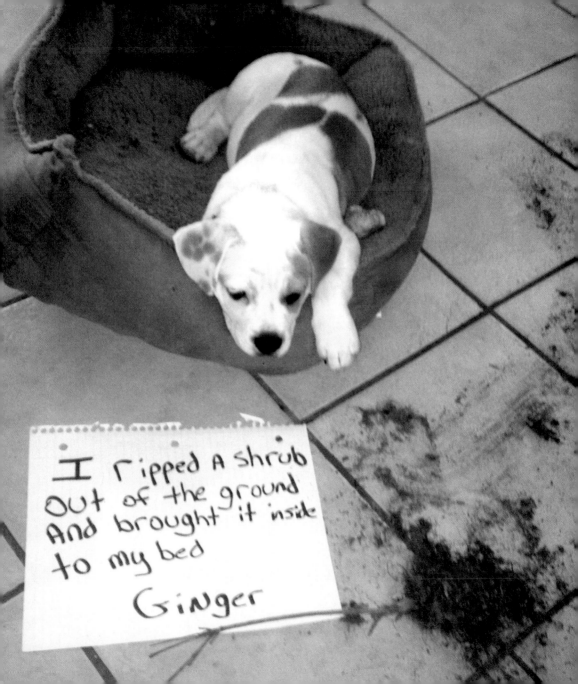

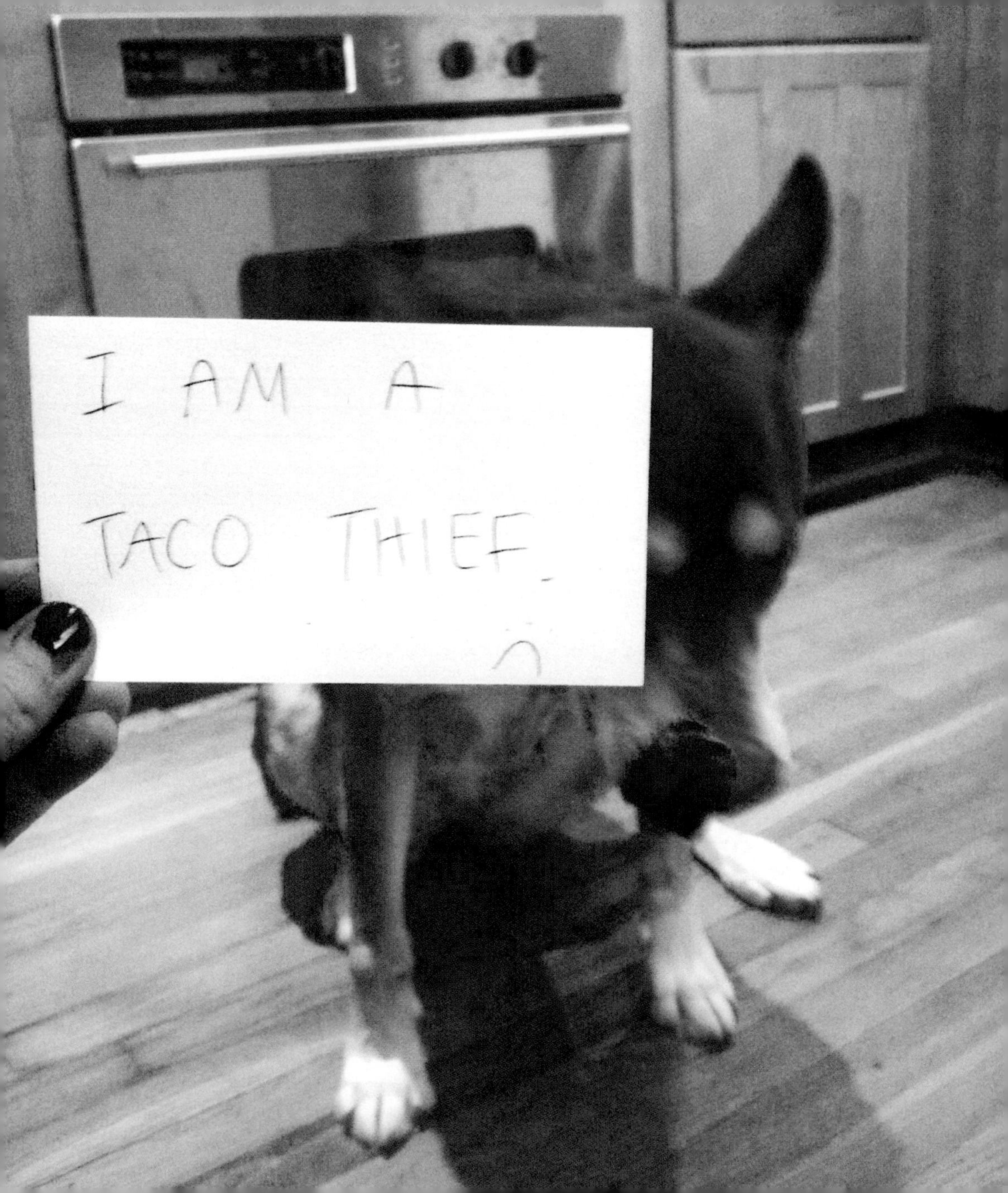
I AM A
TACO THIEF.

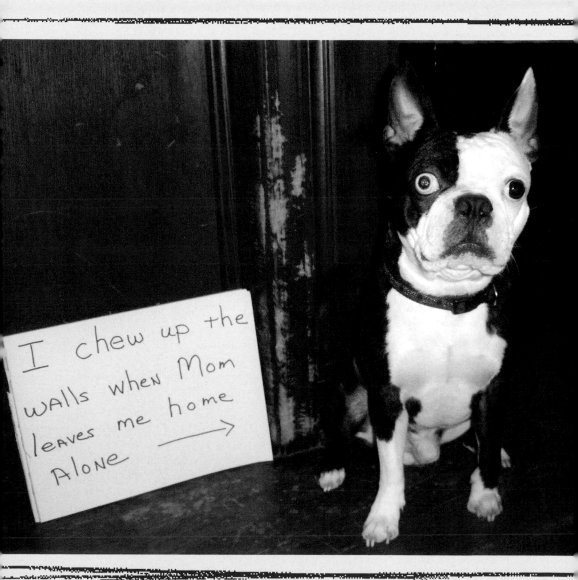

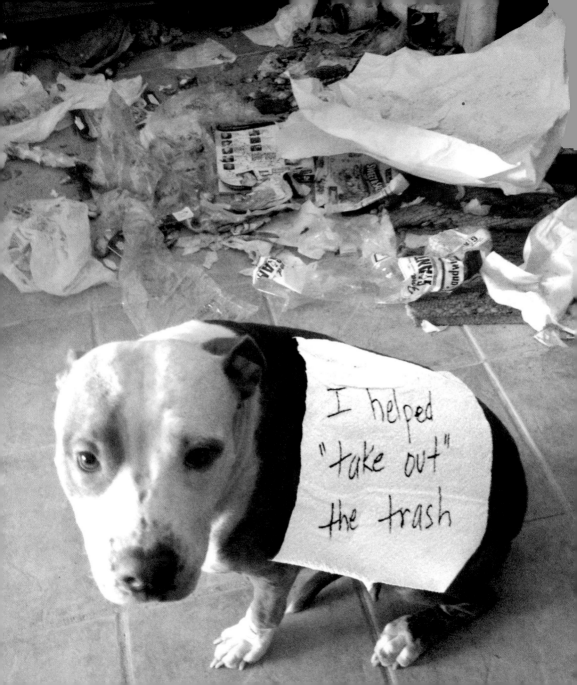

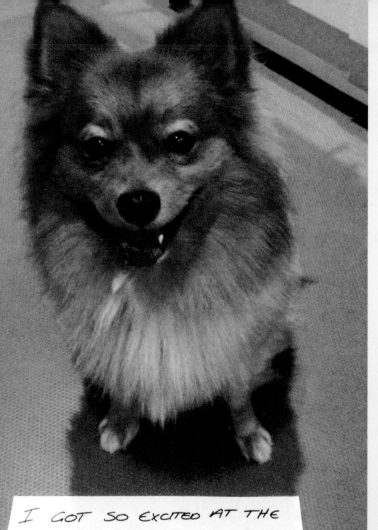

I GOT SO EXCITED AT THE
SNOW, I ATE IT ALL!!

AND GOT BRAINFREEZE ☹

mikey 🐾

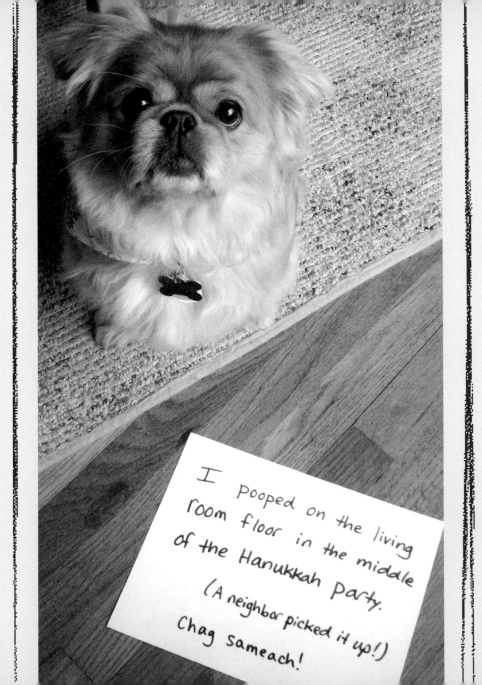

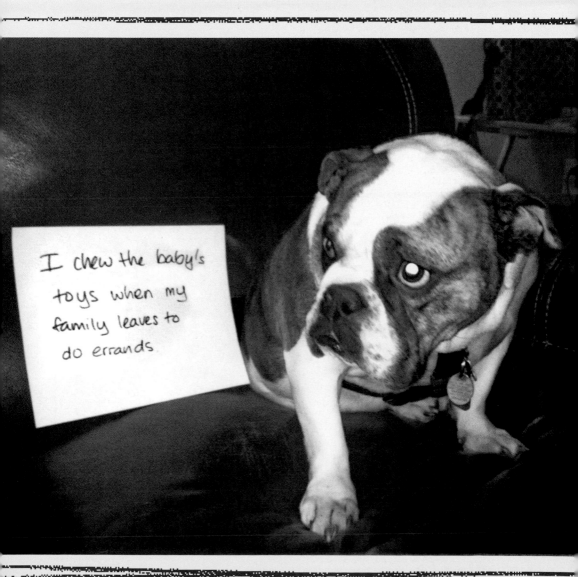

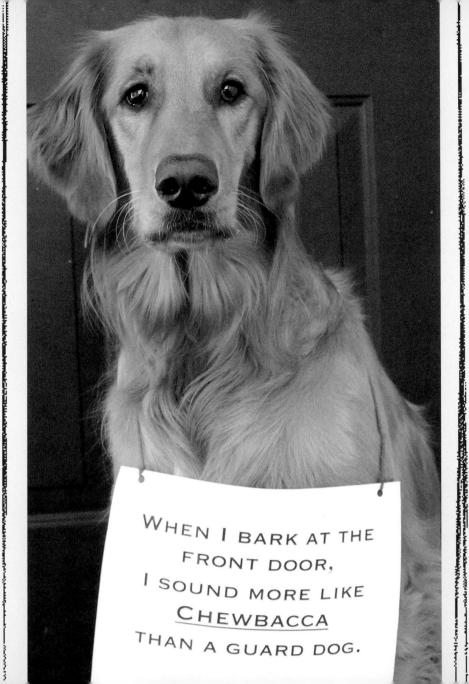

WHEN I BARK AT THE FRONT DOOR, I SOUND MORE LIKE <u>CHEWBACCA</u> THAN A GUARD DOG.

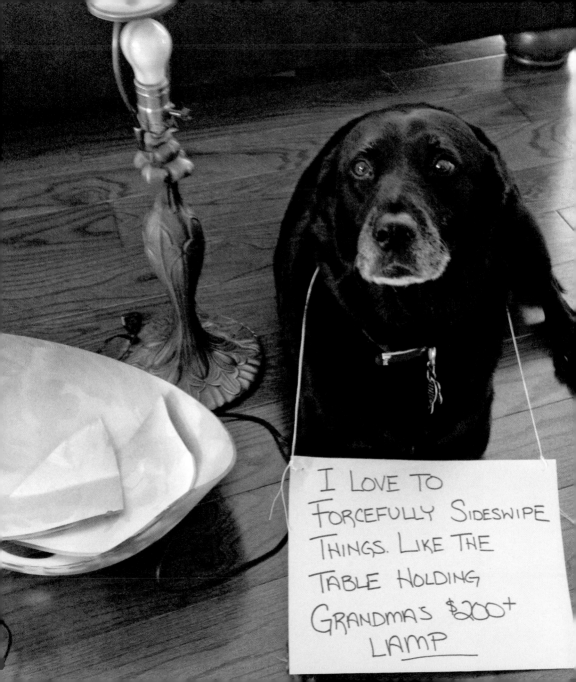

I LOVE TO FORCEFULLY SIDESWIPE THINGS. LIKE THE TABLE HOLDING GRANDMA'S $200+ LAMP

I stole a breakfast sausage off mom's plate. It was delicious. She wasn't looking.

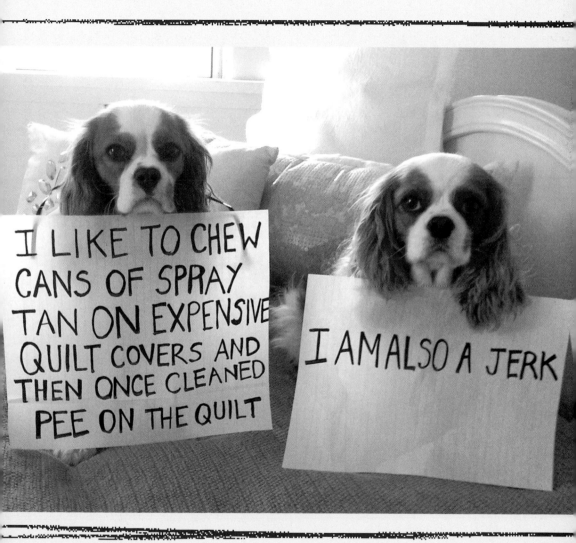

I LIKE TO CHEW CANS OF SPRAY TAN ON EXPENSIVE QUILT COVERS AND THEN ONCE CLEANED PEE ON THE QUILT

I AM ALSO A JERK

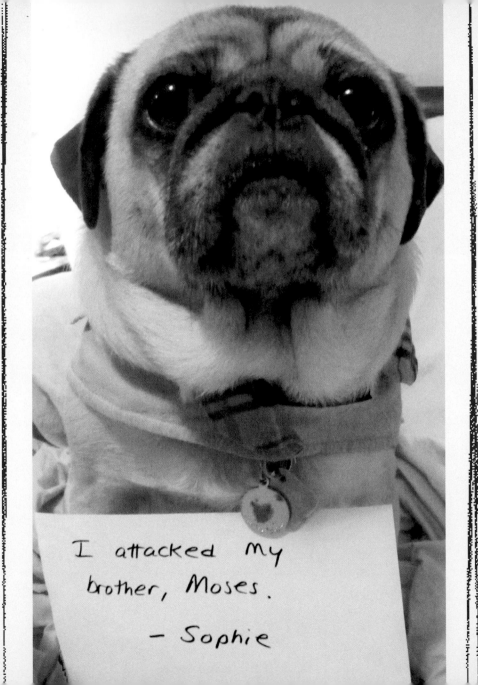

I attacked my brother, Moses.

- Sophie

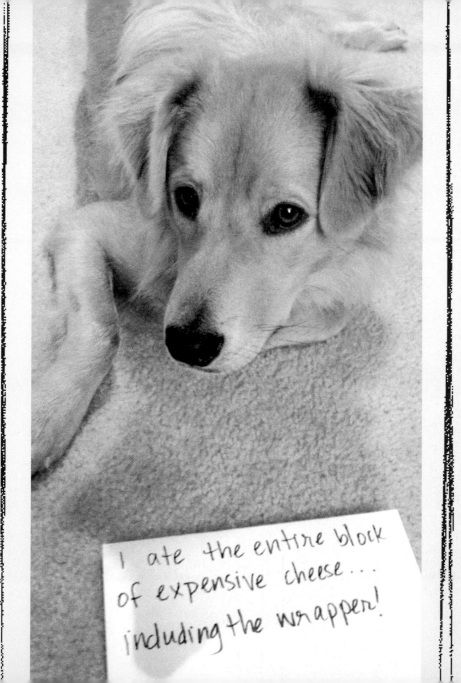

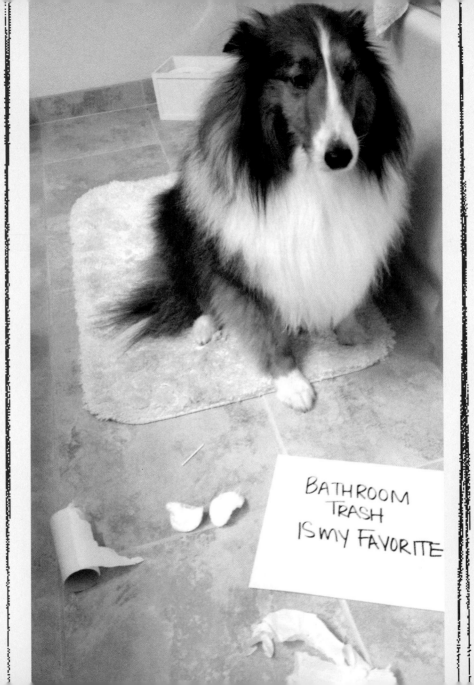

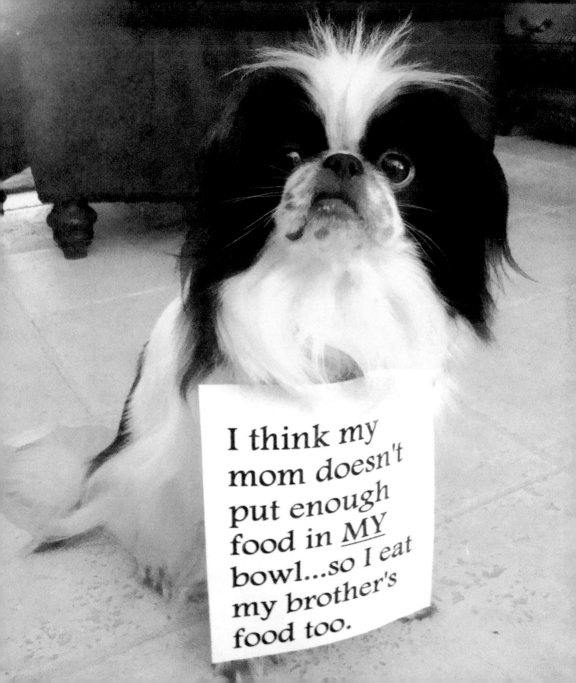

I think my
mom doesn't
put enough
food in MY
bowl...so I eat
my brother's
food too.

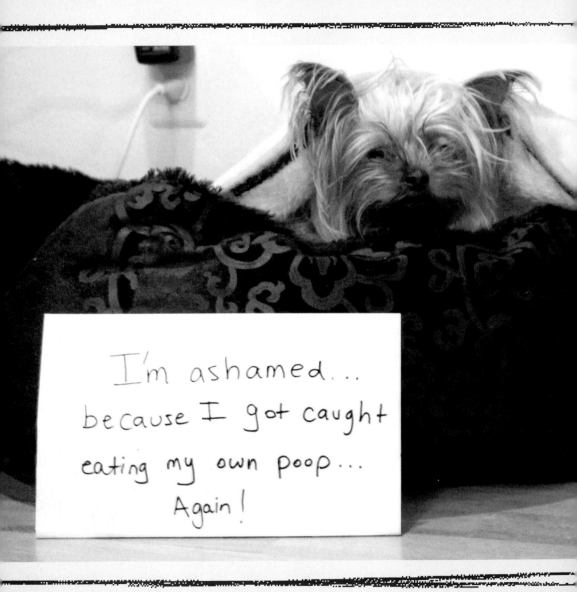

I'm ashamed...
because I got caught
eating my own poop...
Again!

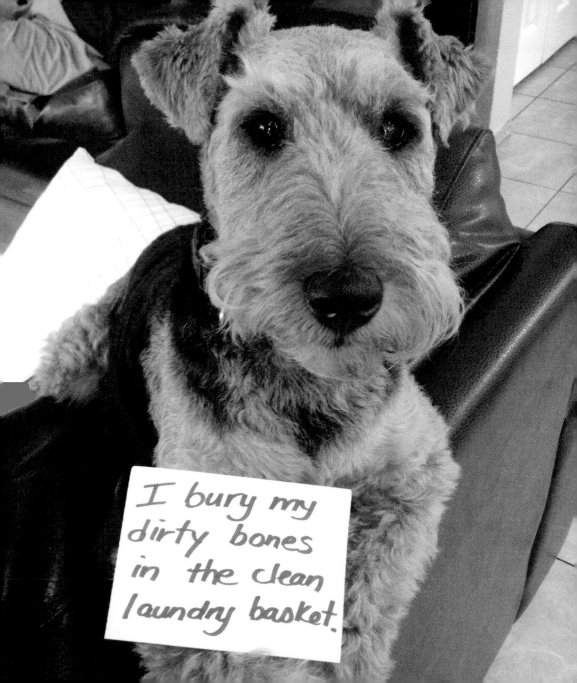

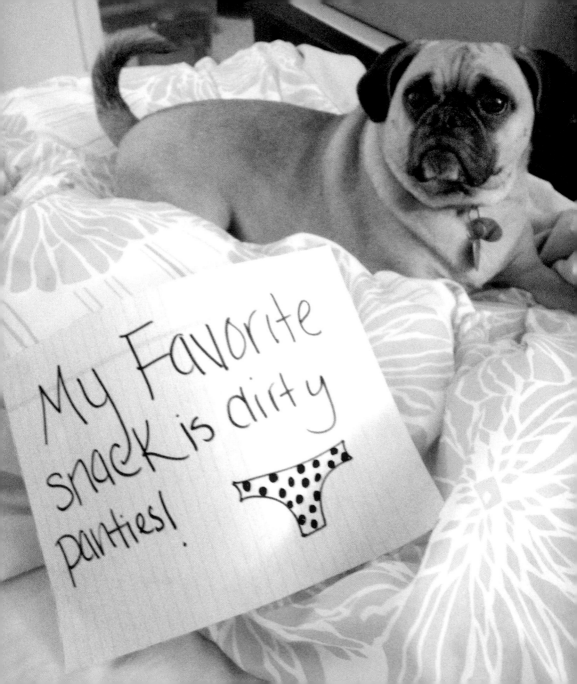

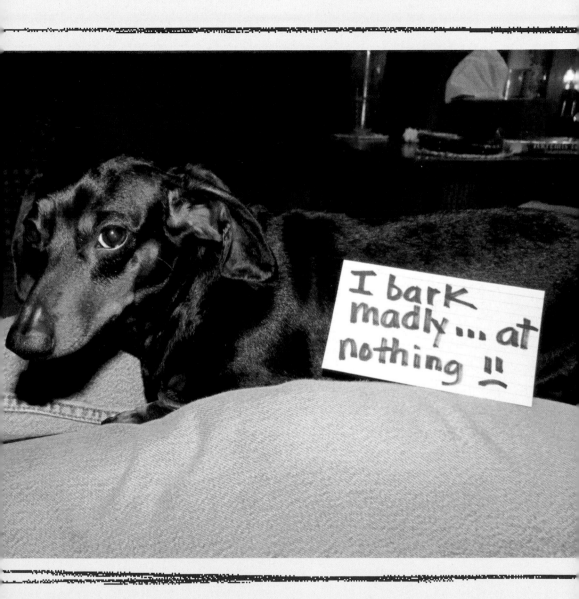

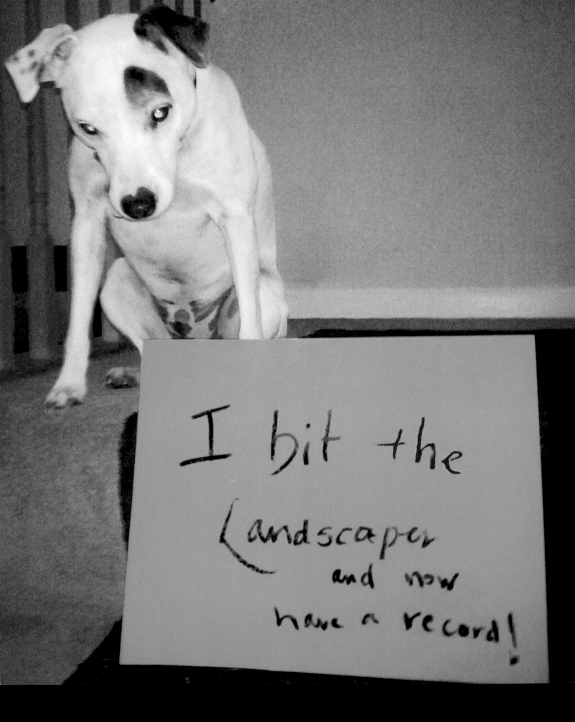

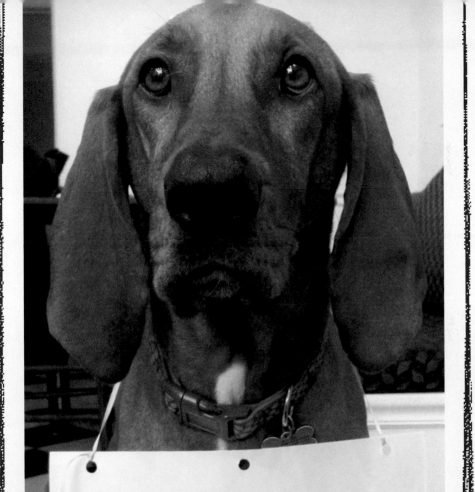

I ate nine red velvet
cupcakes.
Including the paper.
They were delicious.

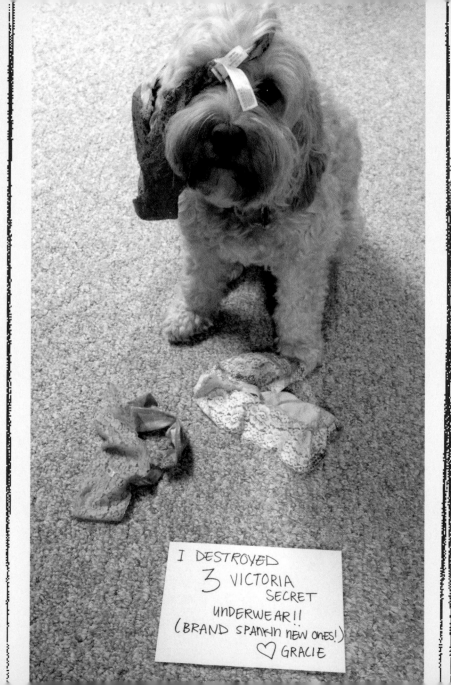

I DESTROYED
3 VICTORIA
SECRET
UNDERWEAR!!
(BRAND SPANKIN NEW ONES!)
♡ GRACIE

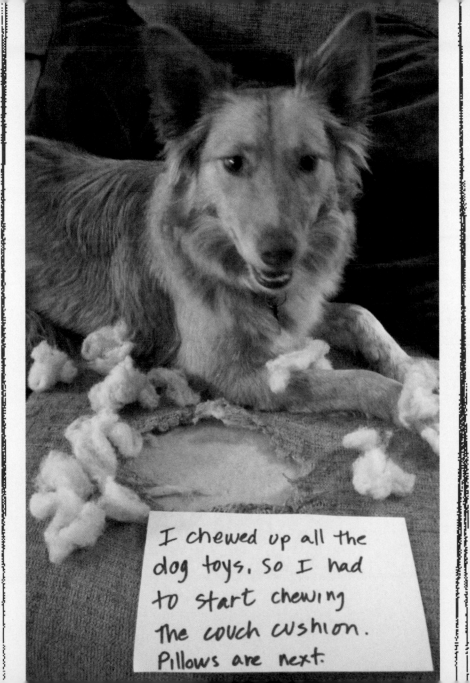

I chewed up all the
dog toys. so I had
to start chewing
the couch cushion.
Pillows are next.

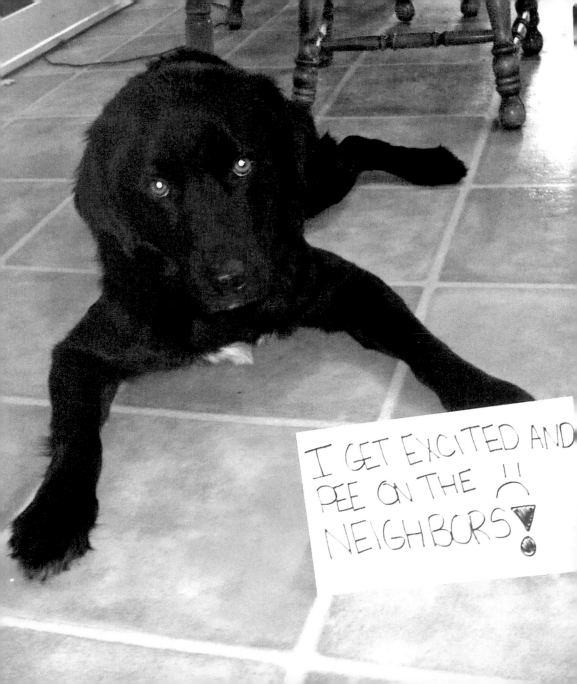

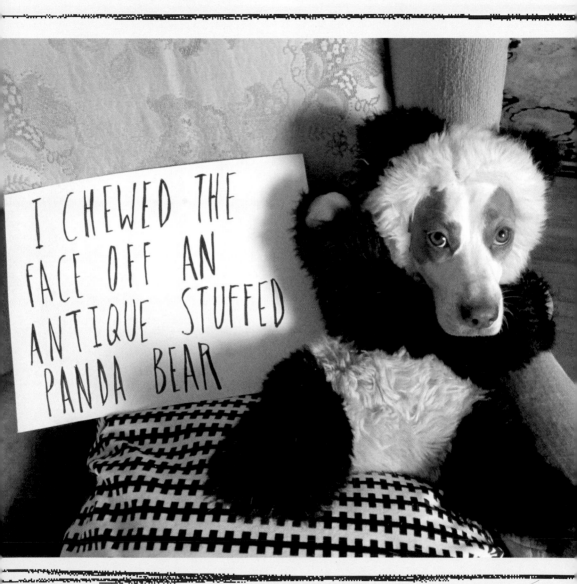

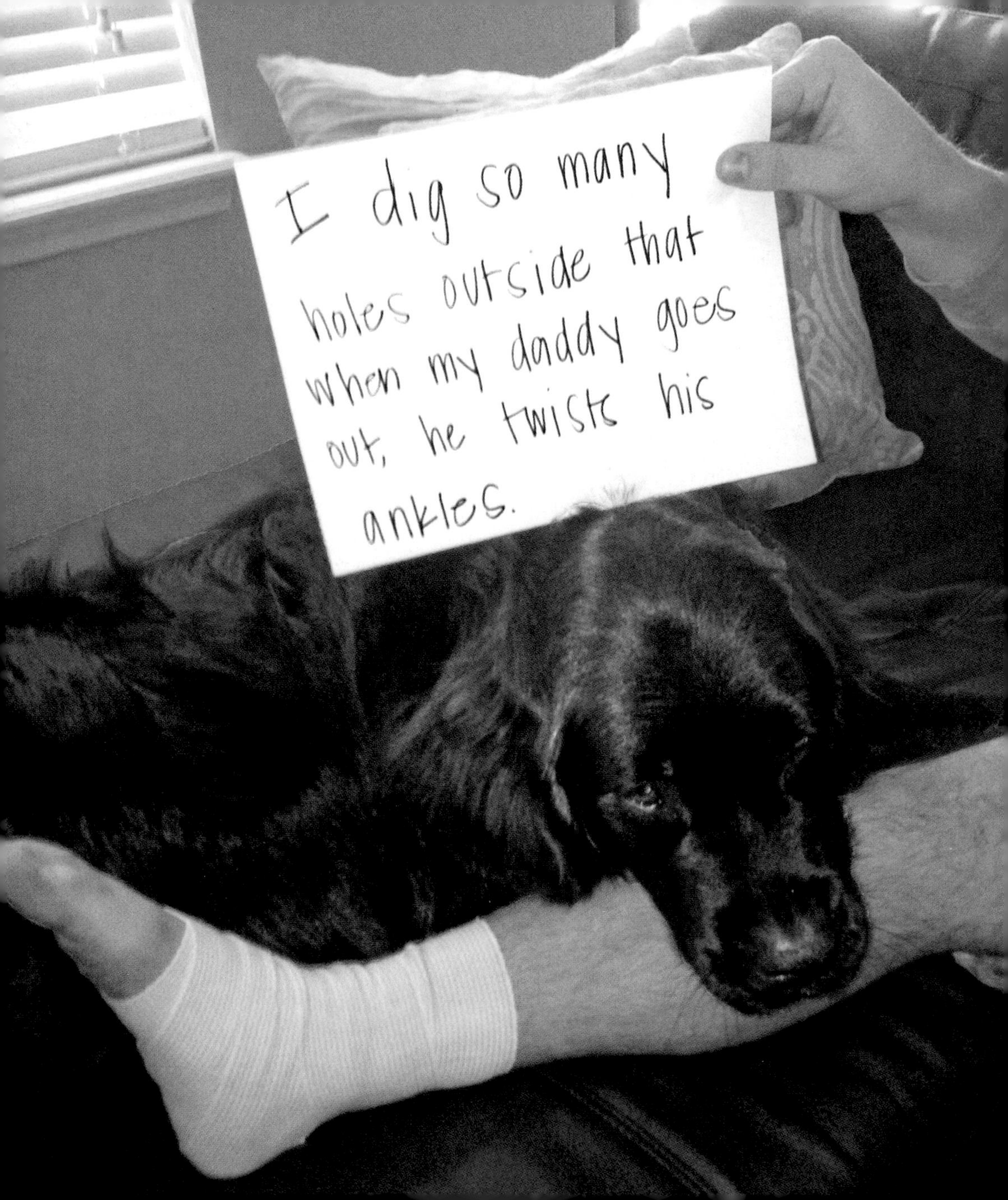
I dig so many
holes outside that
when my daddy goes
out, he twists his
ankles.

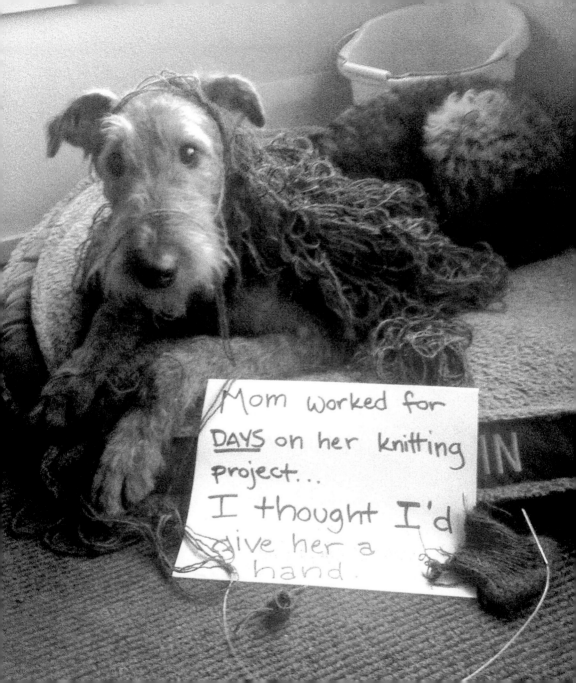

Mom worked for DAYS on her knitting project... I thought I'd give her a hand.

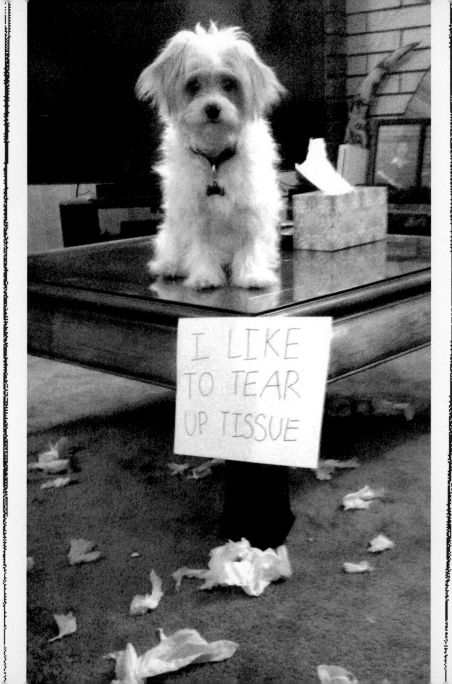

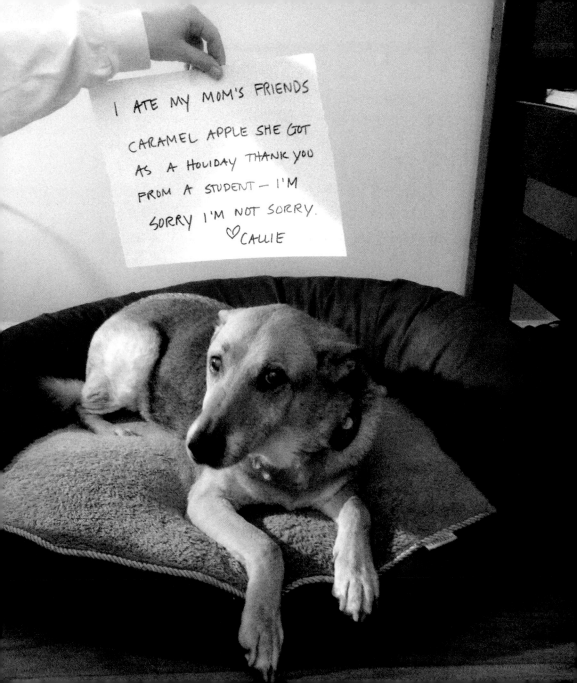

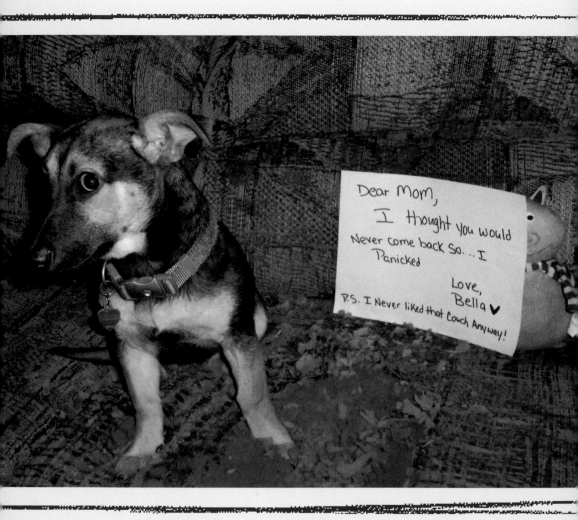

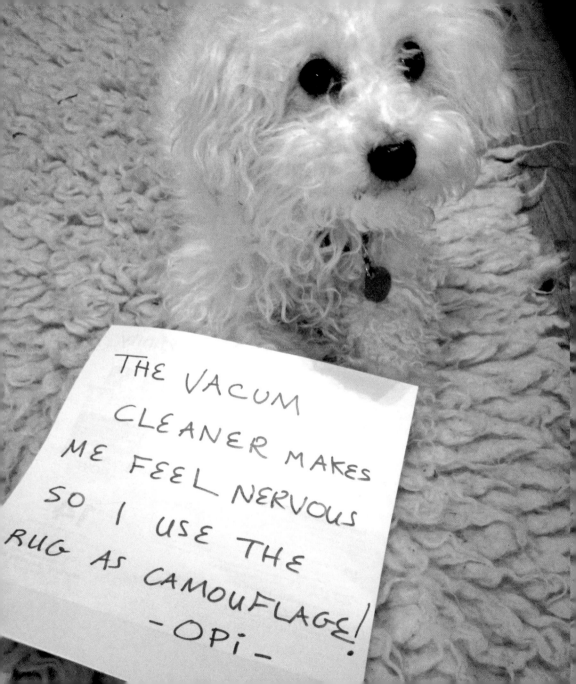

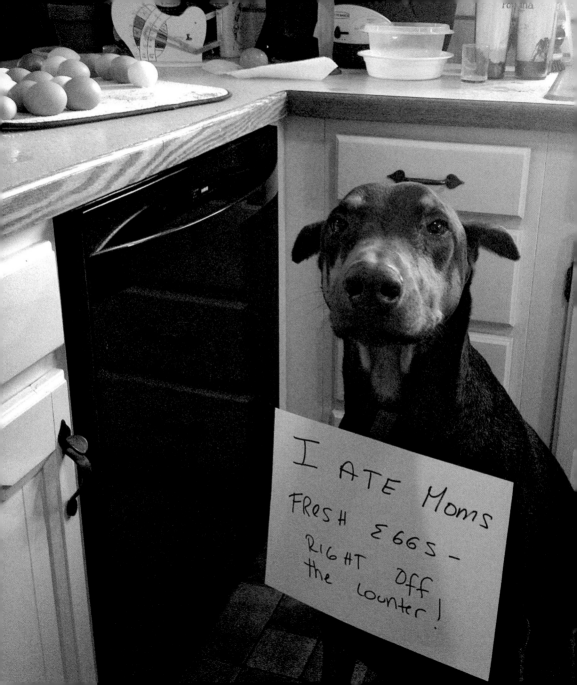

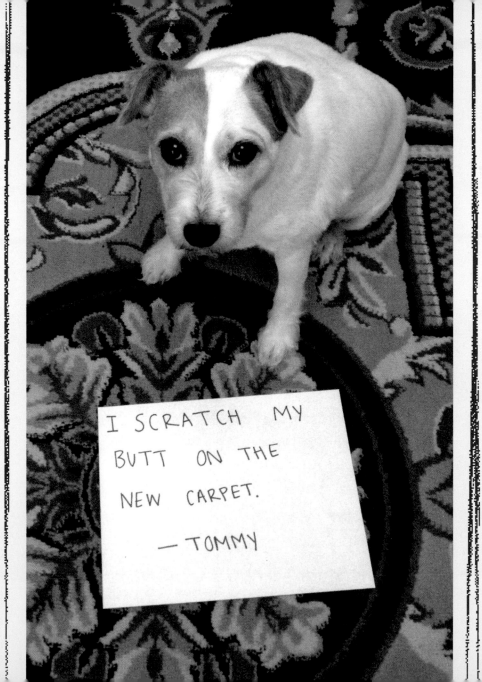

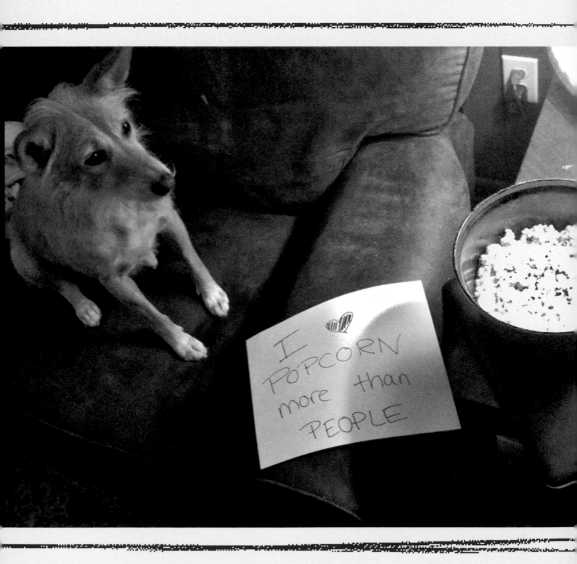

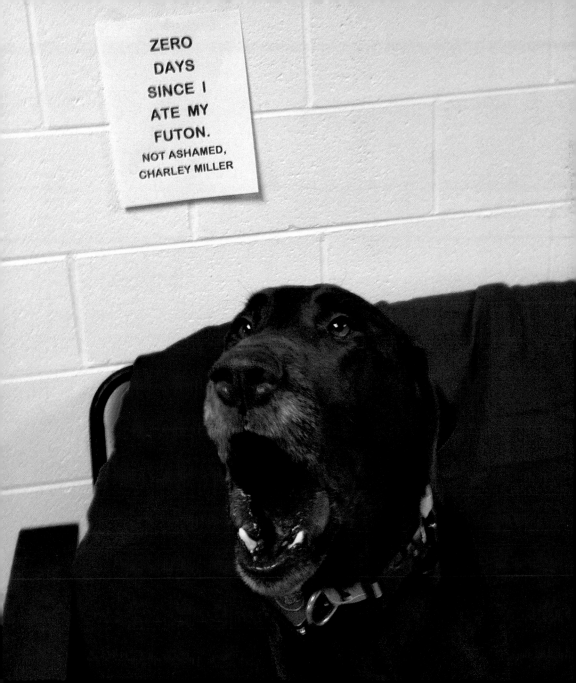

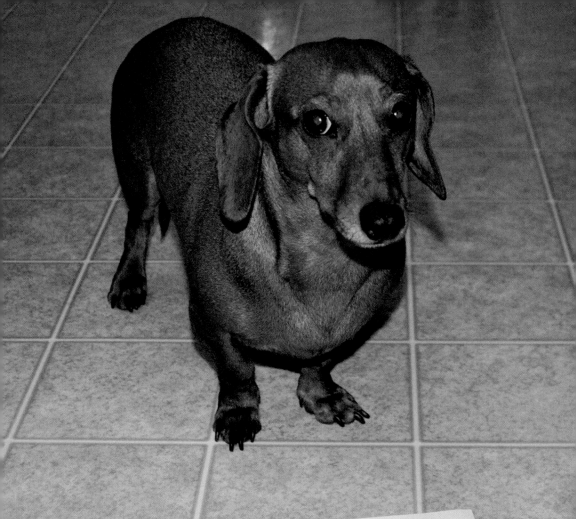

I think my
POOP
is a tasty treat!
-Ginny

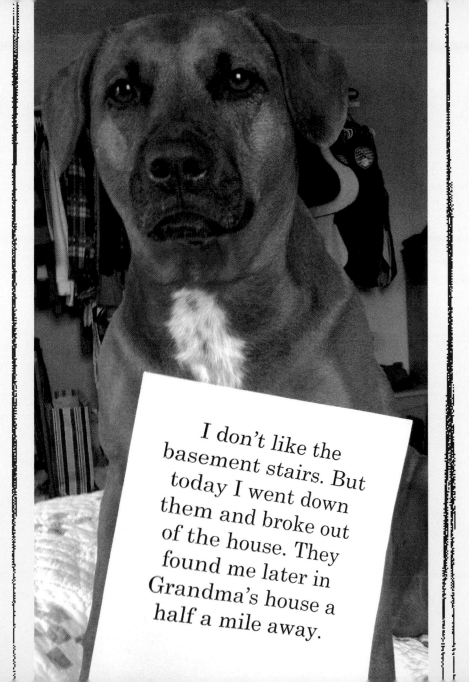

I don't like the basement stairs. But today I went down them and broke out of the house. They found me later in Grandma's house a half a mile away.

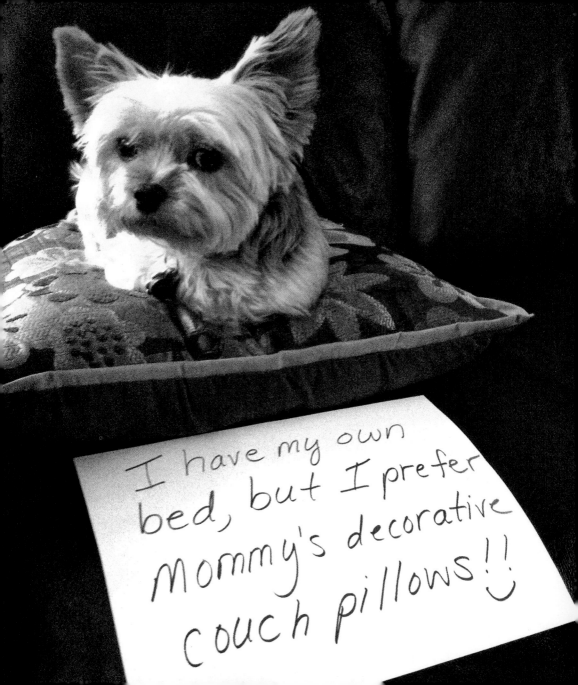

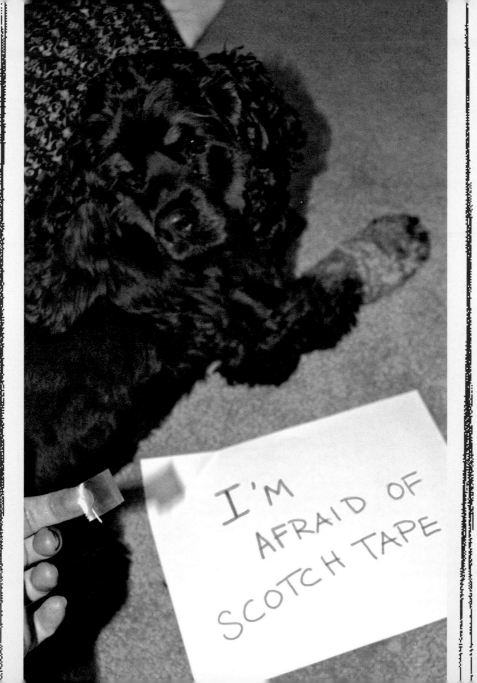

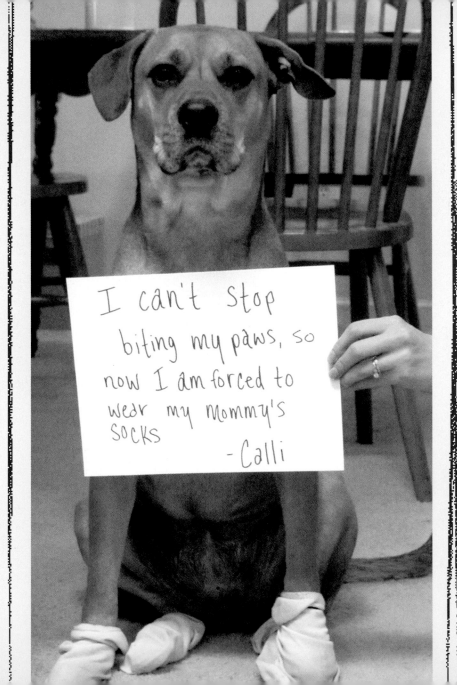

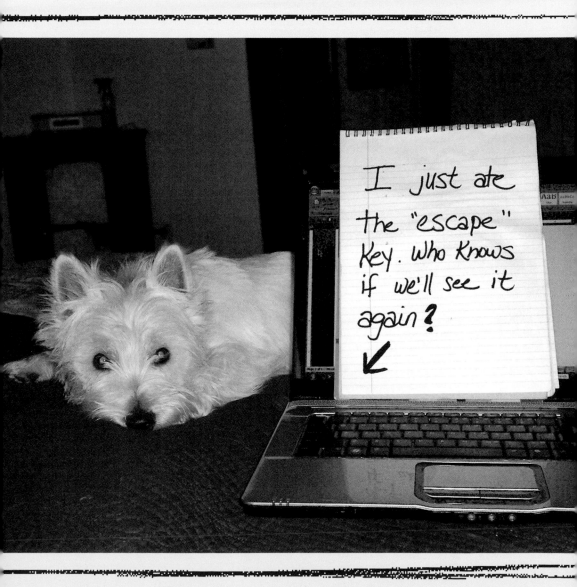

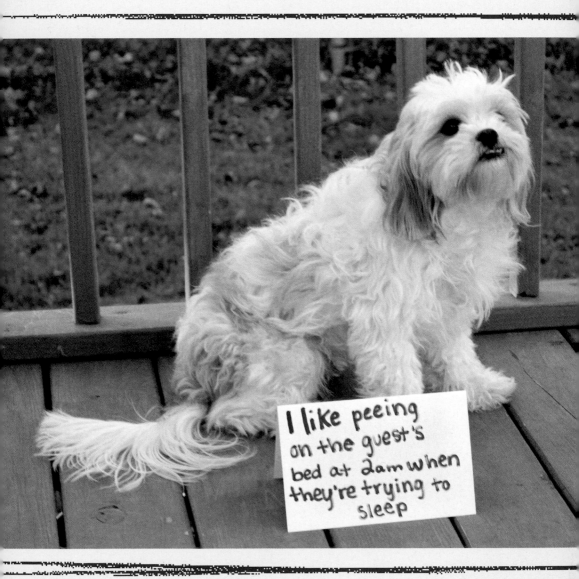

I ATE MY mom's PIE CRUST BEFORE SHE GOT IT IN THE PIE PAN! Happy Thanksgiving

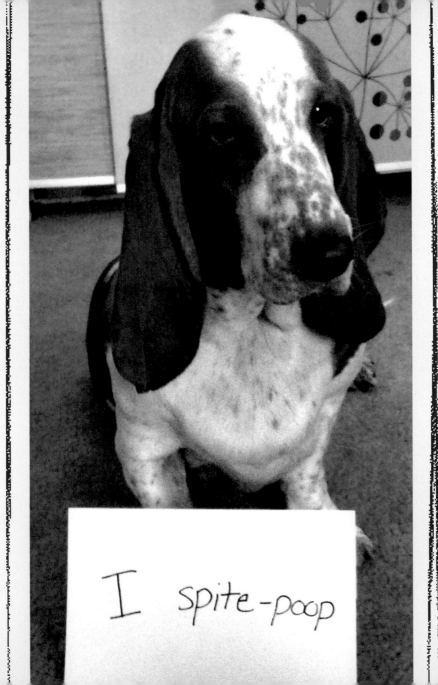

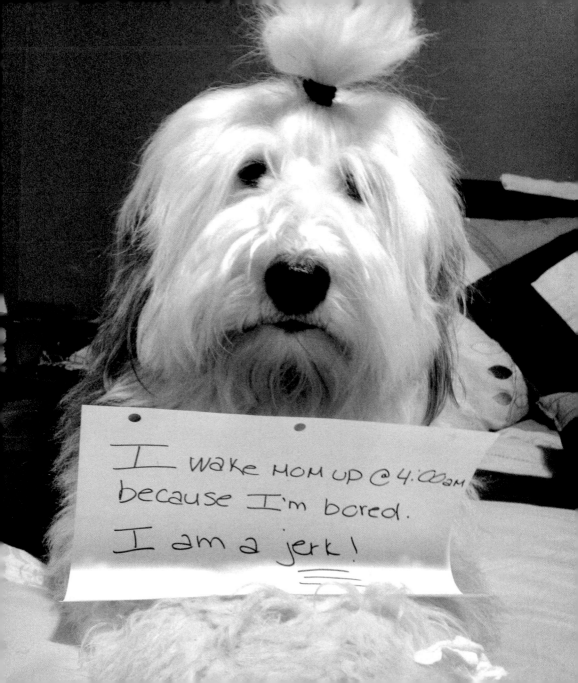

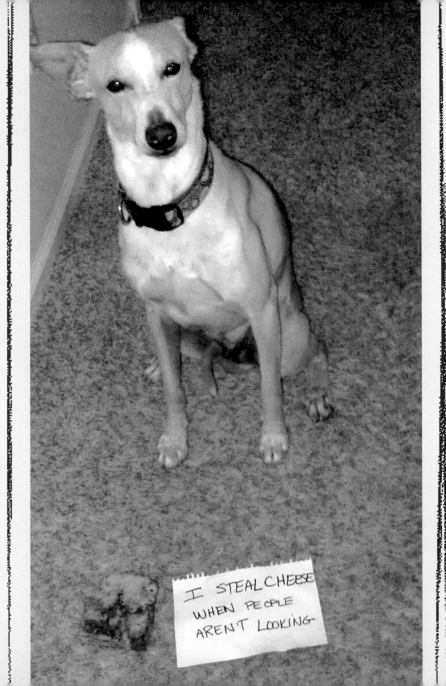

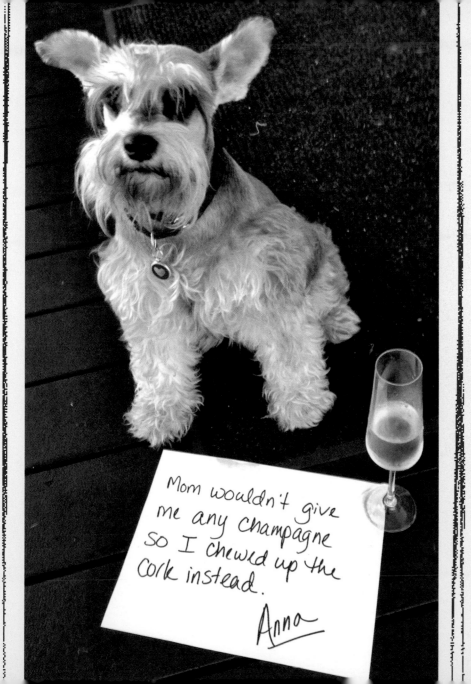

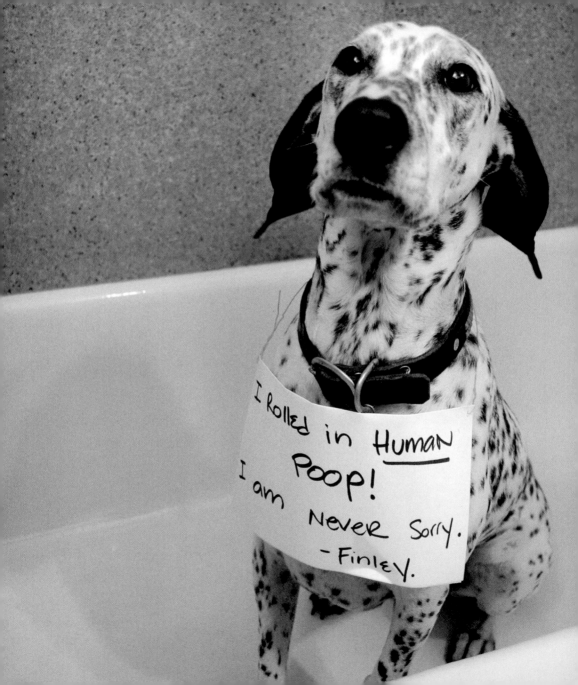

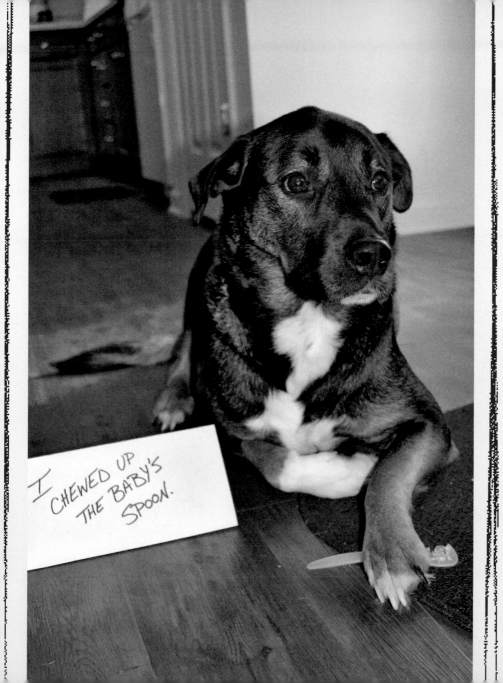

I CHEWED UP THE BABY'S SPOON.

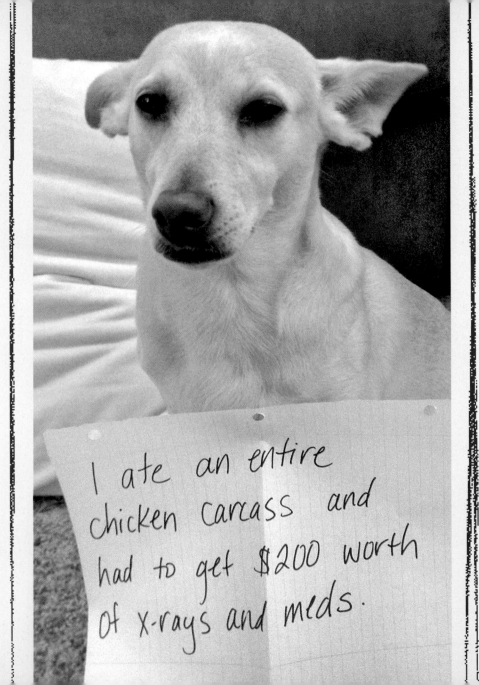

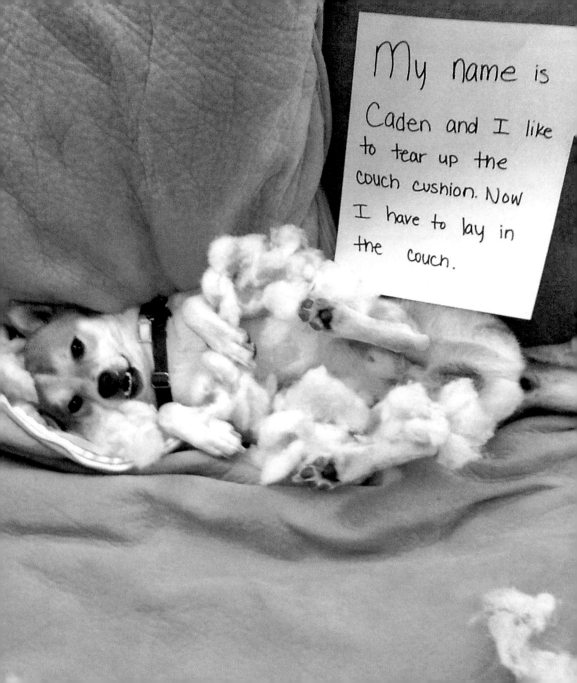

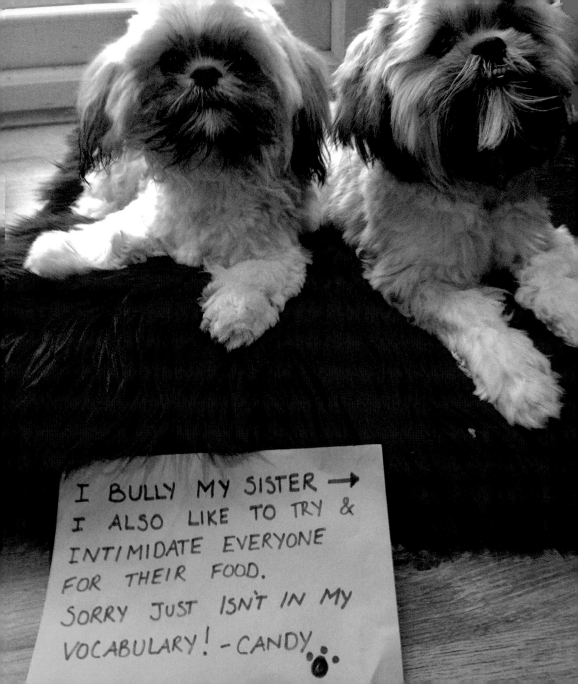

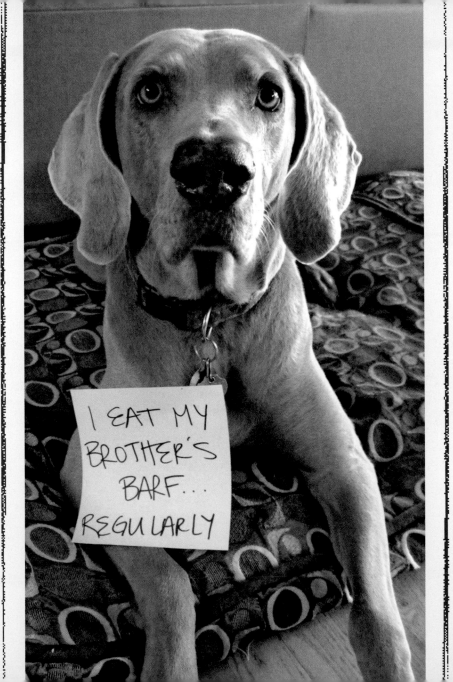

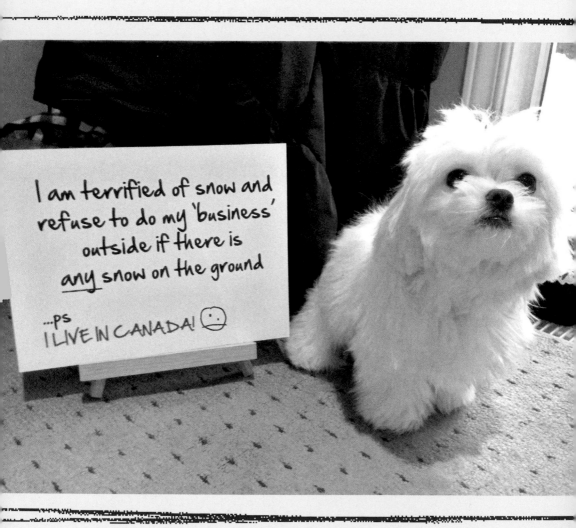

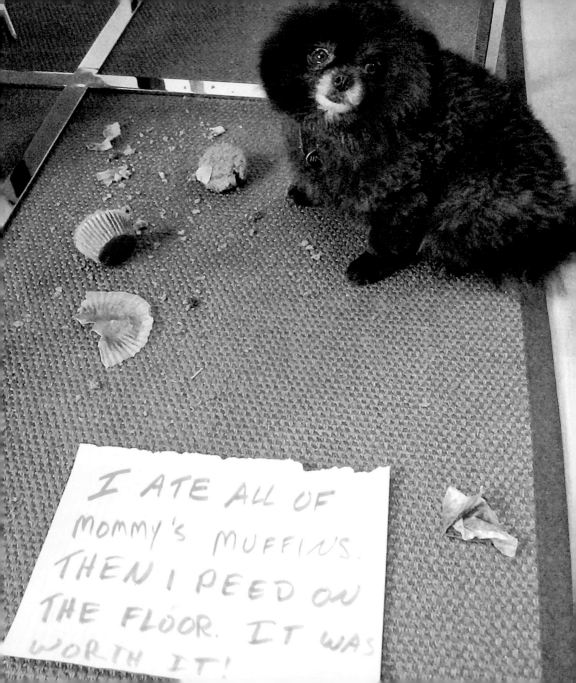

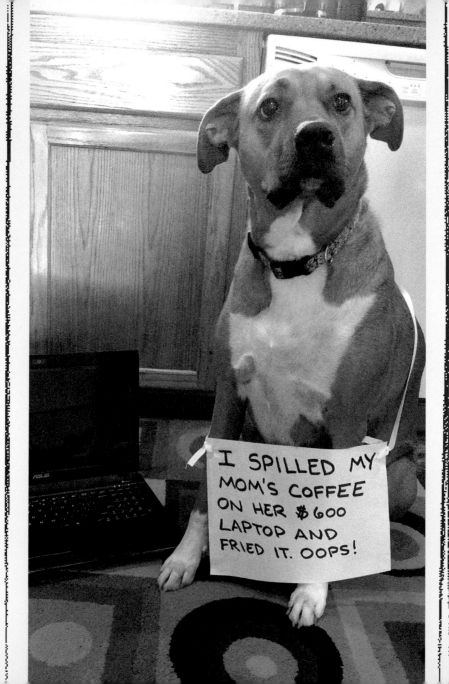

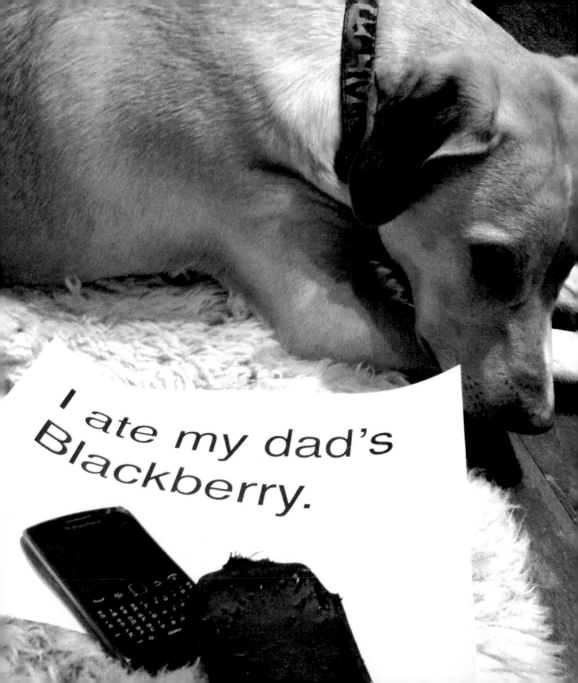

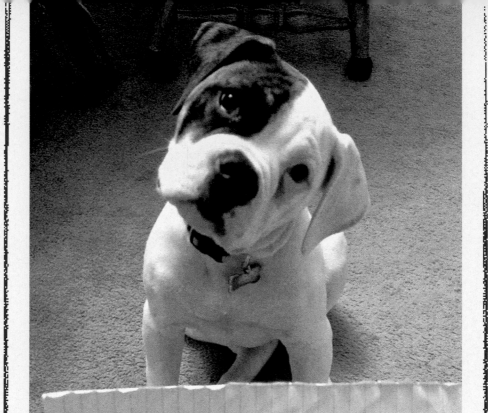

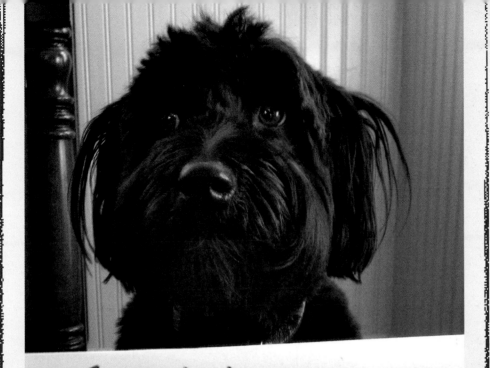

I stole a Stick of butter...
ate it under the
Dining Room table....
and barfed on the
Rug. I ♡ Butter! Stella

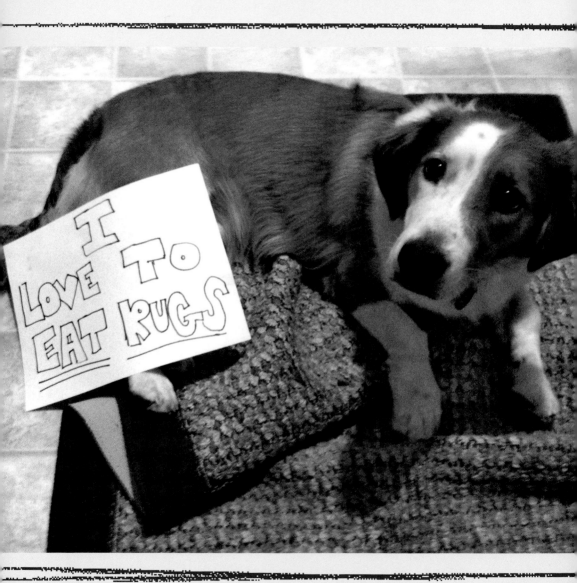

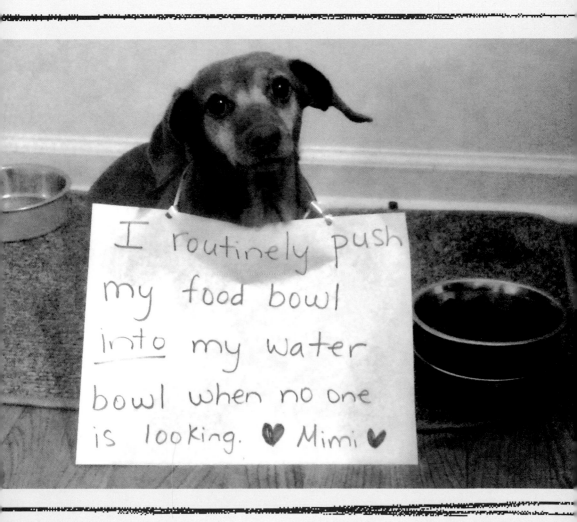

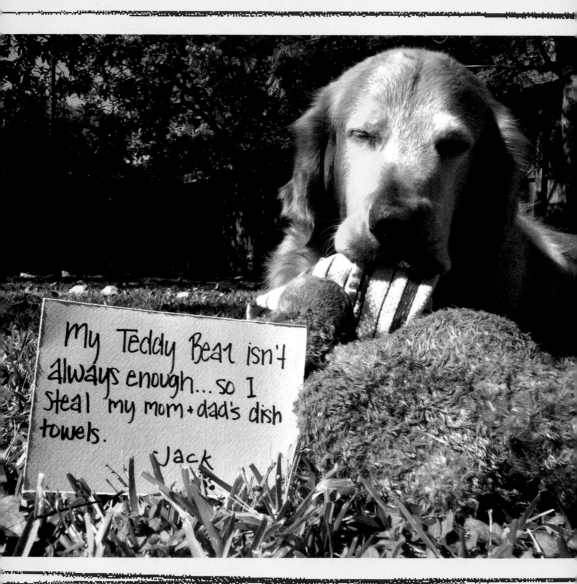

My Teddy Bear isn't always enough...so I steal my mom + dad's dish towels.

Jack

I tear my puppy pad into a bazillion pieces.

__Then__ I pee on it!

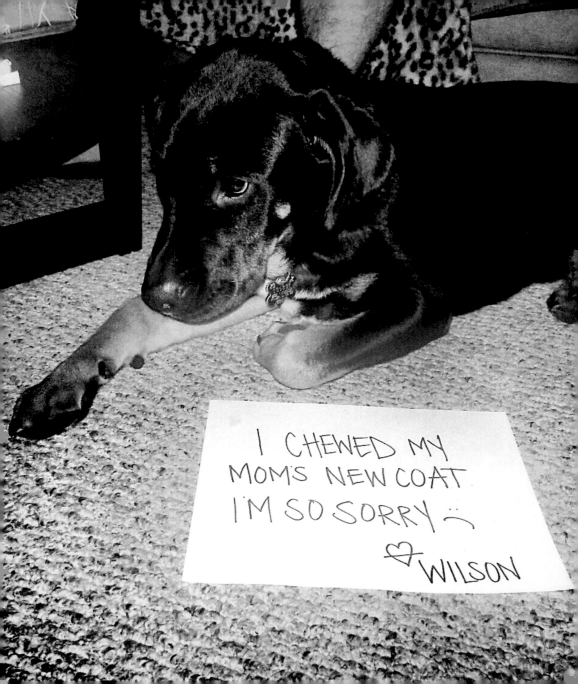

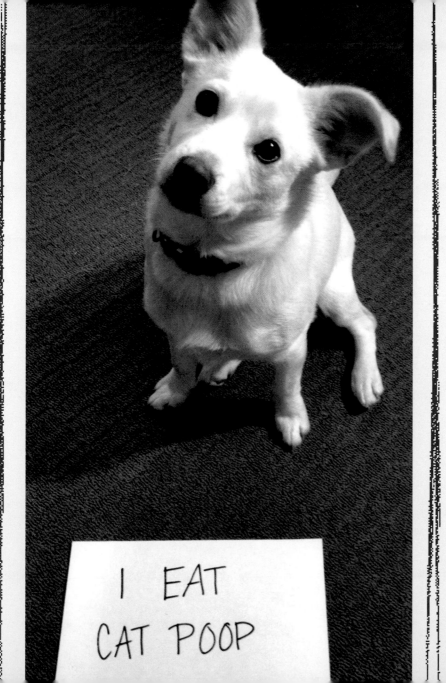

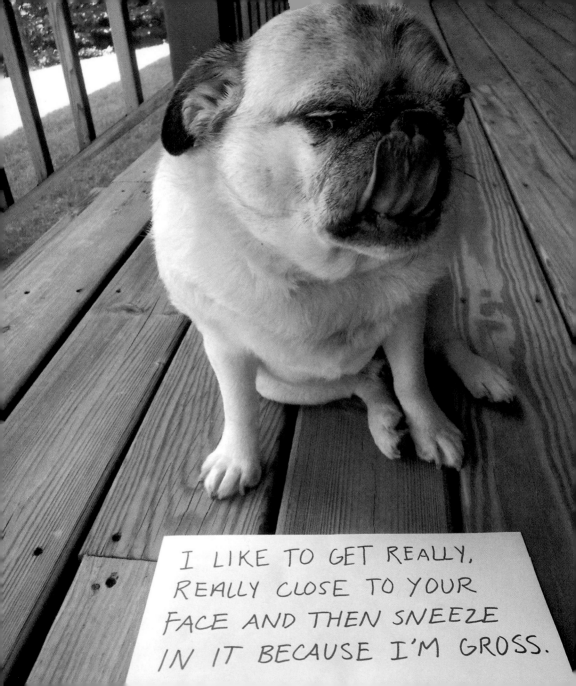

I LIKE TO GET REALLY,
REALLY CLOSE TO YOUR
FACE AND THEN SNEEZE
IN IT BECAUSE I'M GROSS.

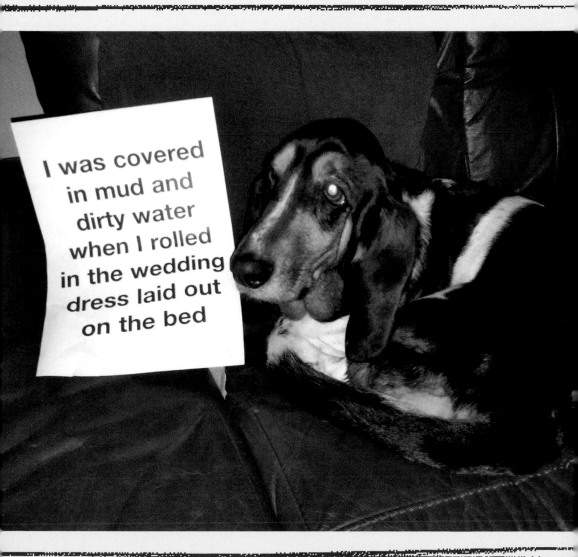

I was covered in mud and dirty water when I rolled in the wedding dress laid out on the bed

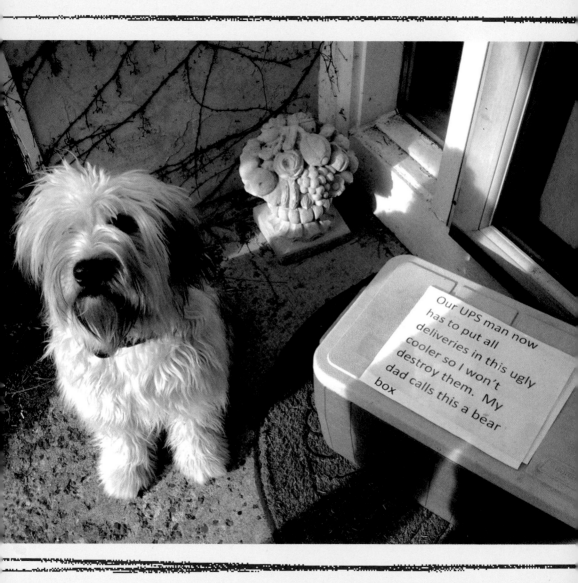

Our UPS man now has to put all deliveries in this ugly cooler so I won't destroy them. My dad calls this a bear box

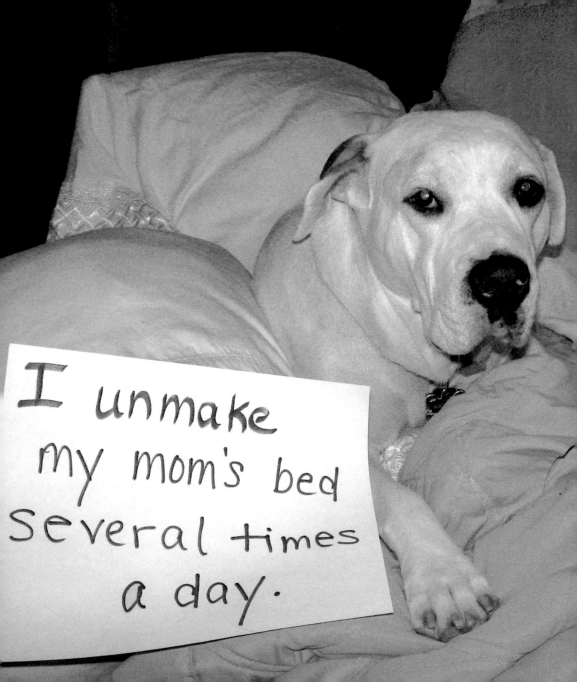

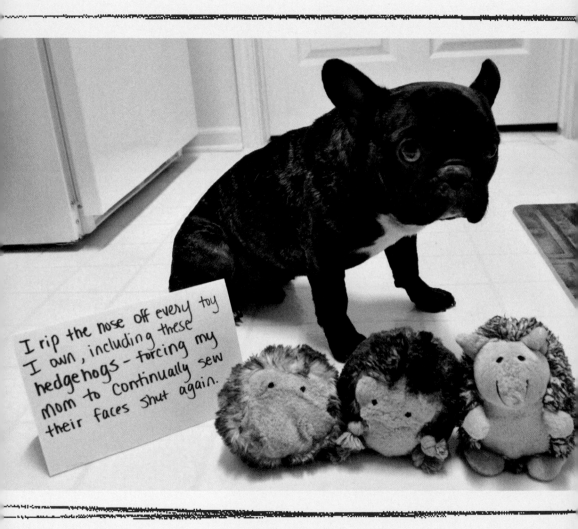

I rip the nose off every toy I own, including these hedgehogs - forcing my mom to continually sew their faces shut again.

140

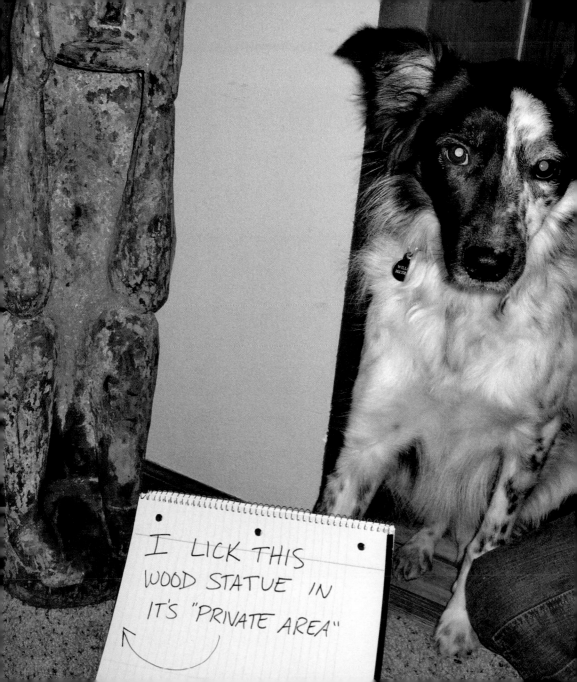

I ATE...INHALED MY MOM'S 10pc & FRIES AFTER SHE WAS NICE & TOOK ME FOR A RIDE

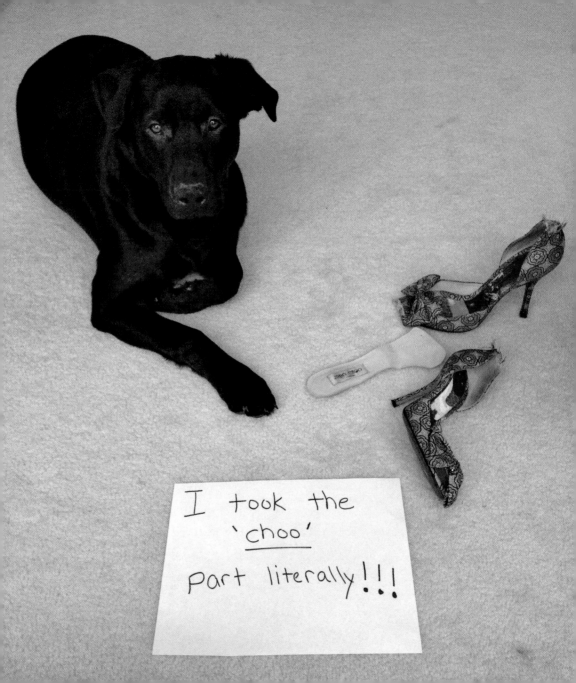

This is what happens when you relentlessly pursue the contents of the Dutch oven & somehow knock it off the (cold) stovetop onto your foot. THREE BROKEN METATARSALS (IT WAS WORTH IT!)

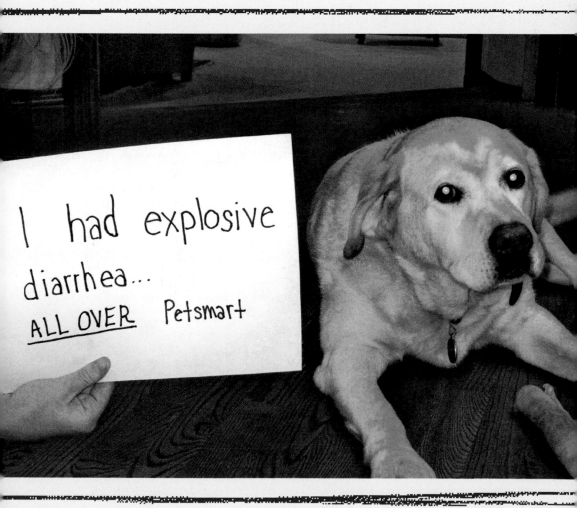

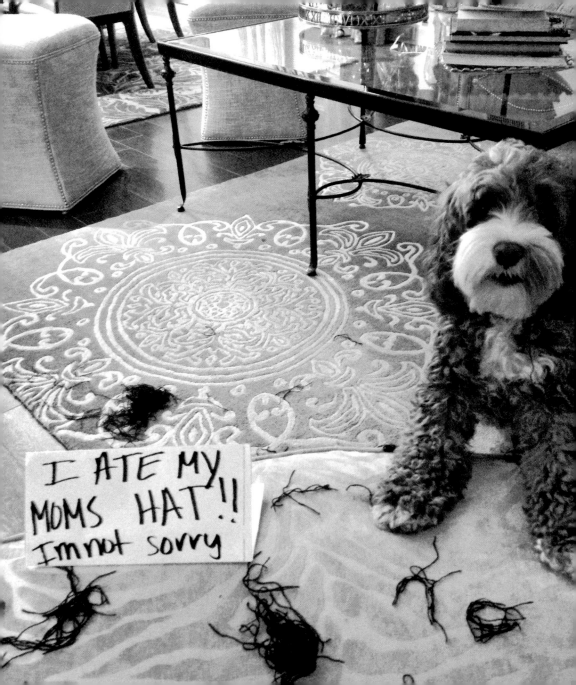

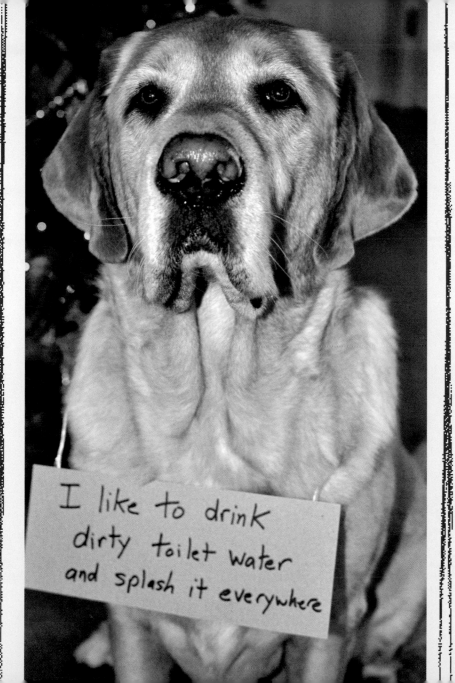

I like to drink
dirty toilet water
and splash it everywhere

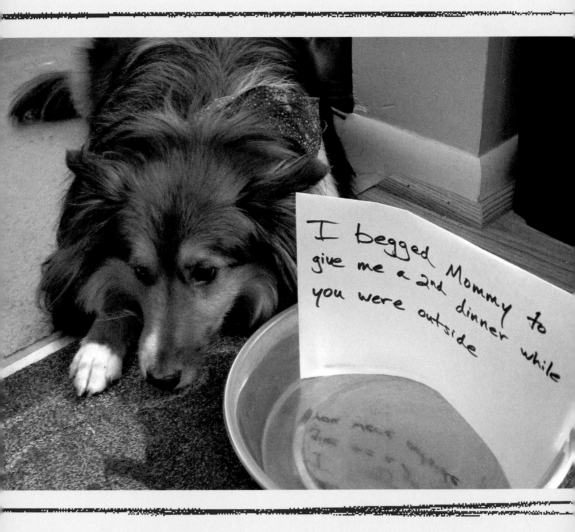

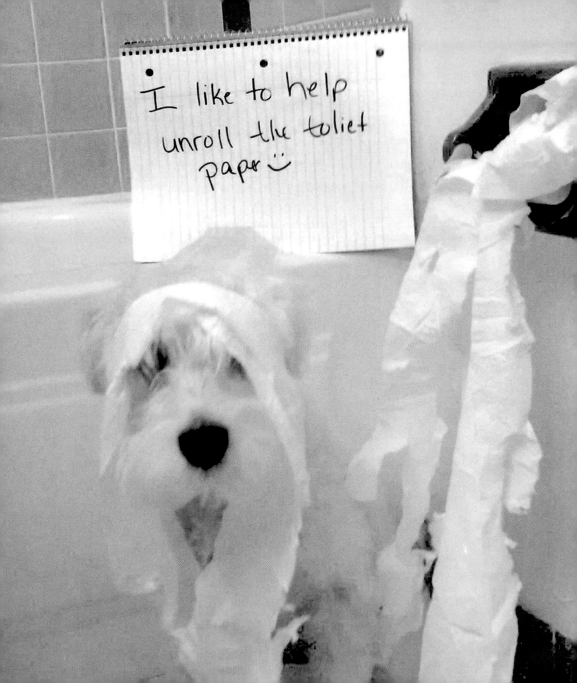

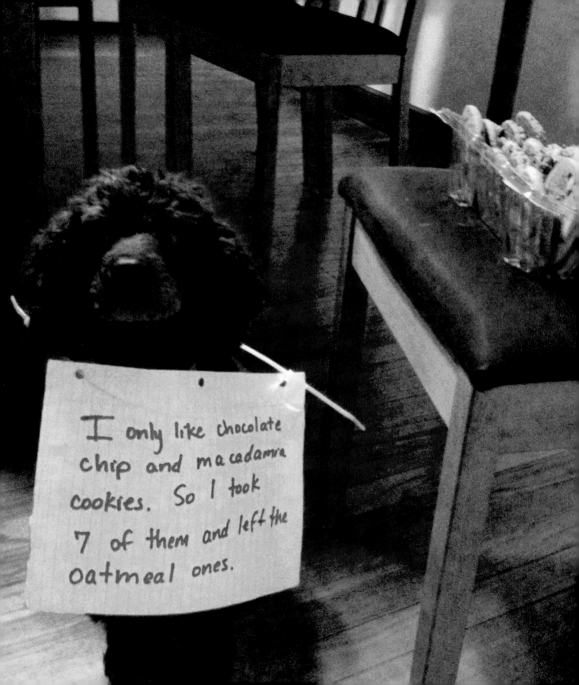

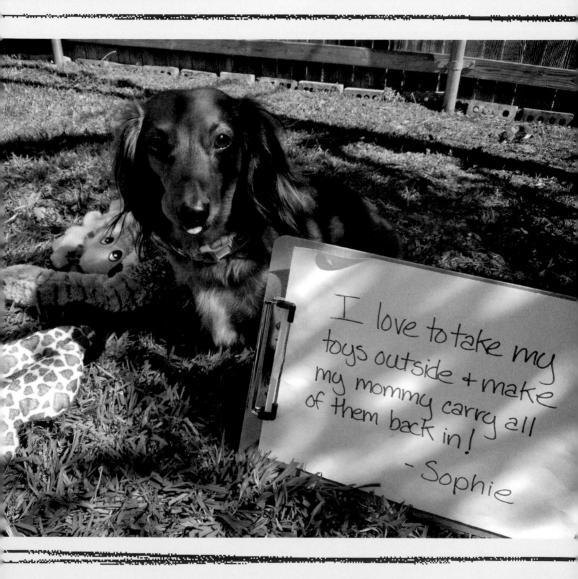

I love to take my toys outside + make my mommy carry all of them back in!
— Sophie

I have an affinity for Kitty litter. The proof is on my nose.
♡Ginny

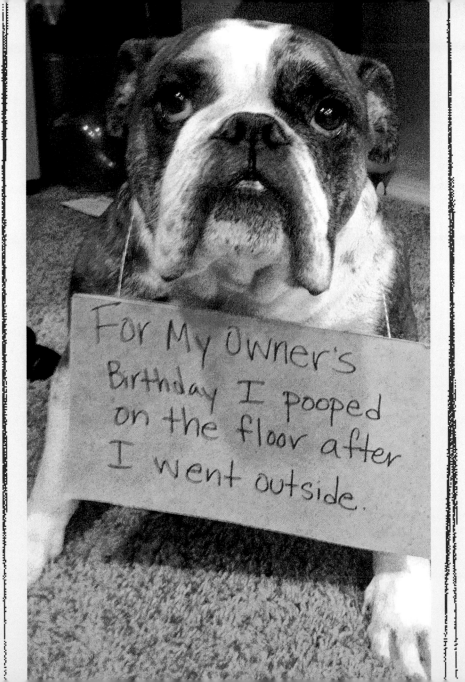

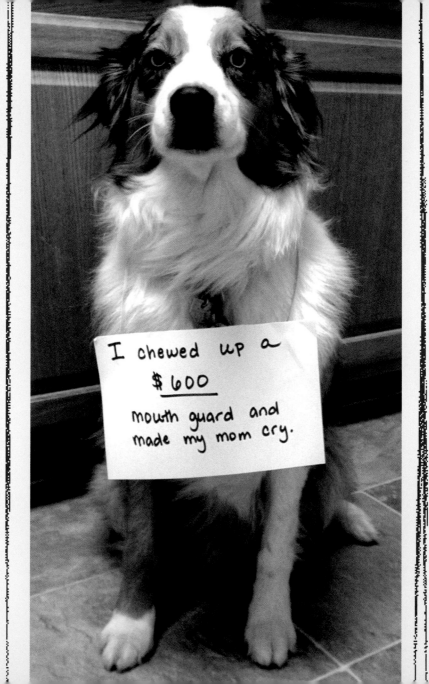

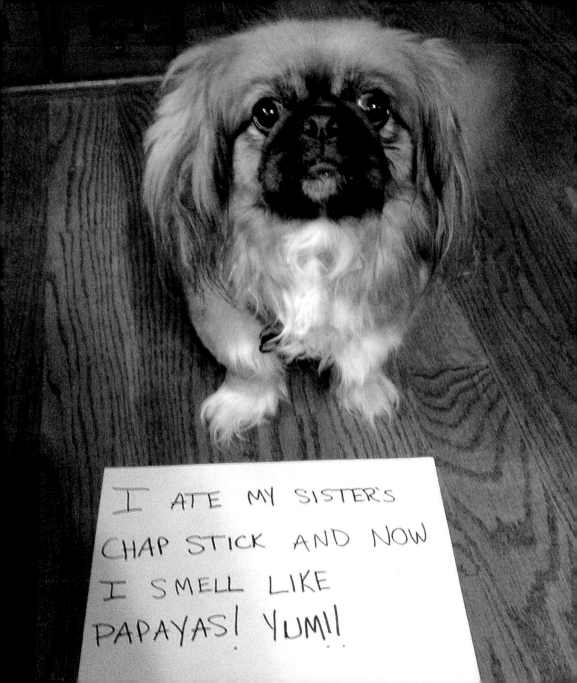

I ATE MY SISTER'S
CHAP STICK AND NOW
I SMELL LIKE
PAPAYAS! YUM!!

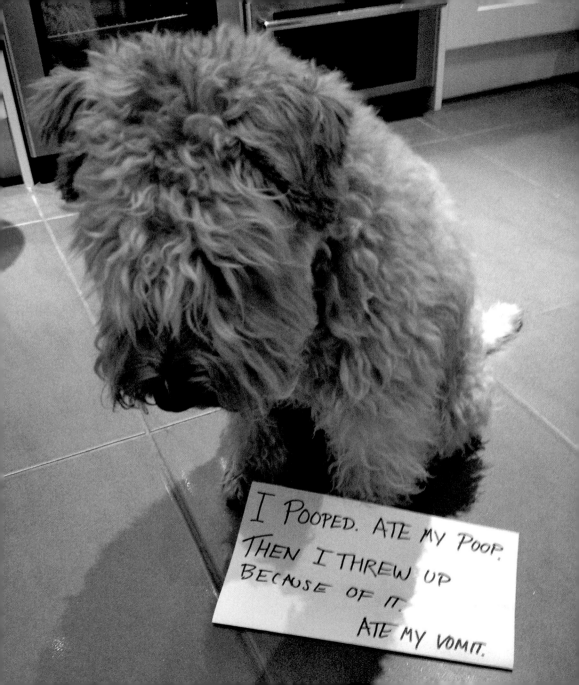

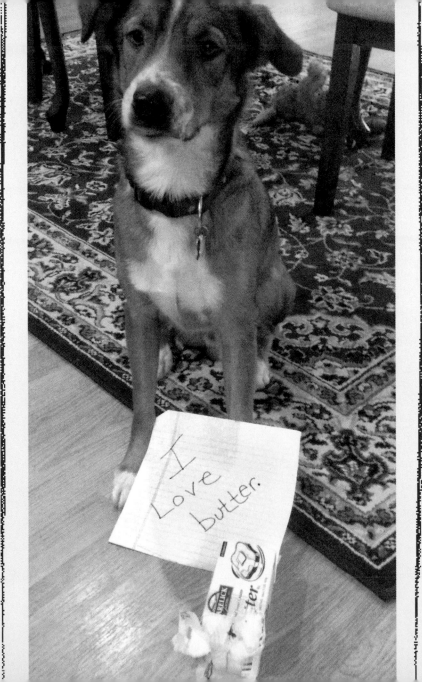

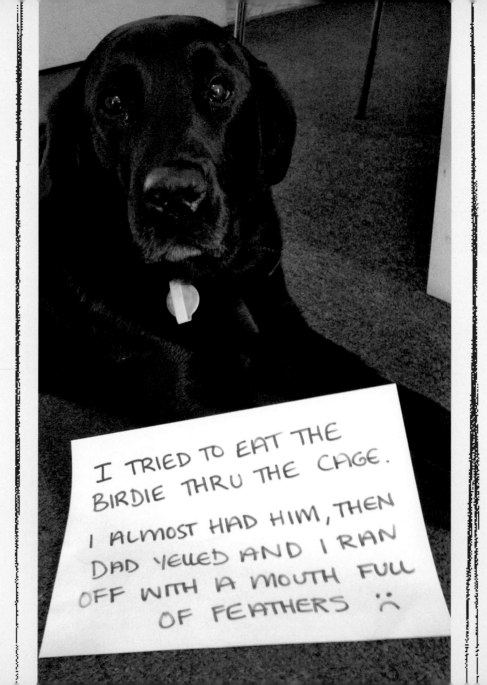

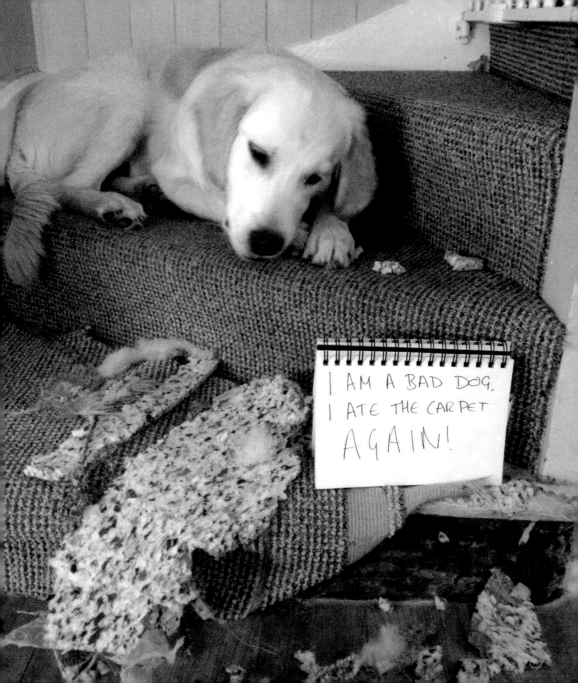

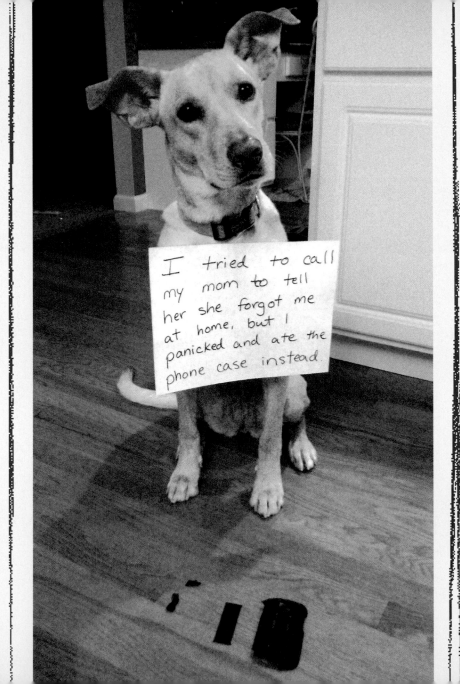

I tried to call my mom to tell her she forgot me at home, but I panicked and ate the phone case instead.

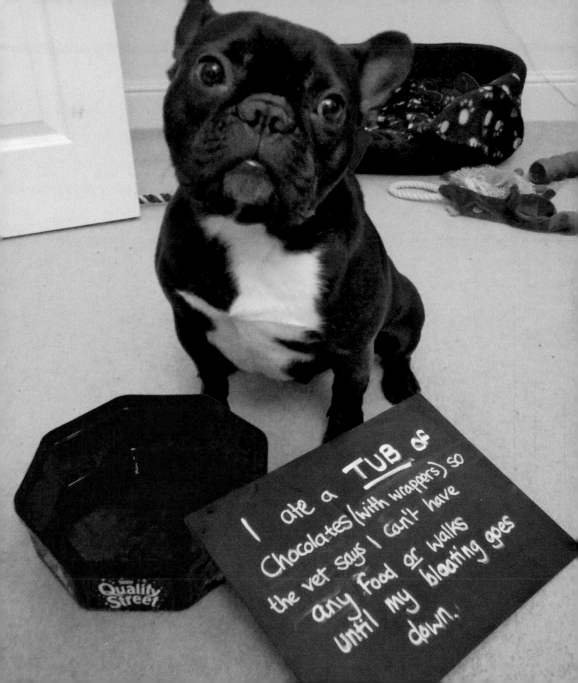

I ate a TUB of Chocolates (with wrappers) so the vet says I can't have any food or walks until my bloating goes down.

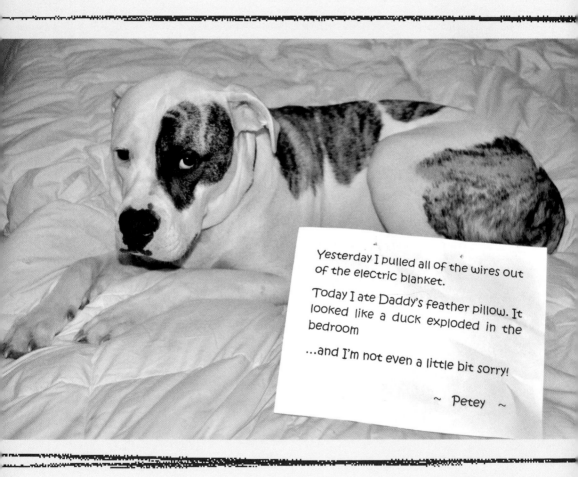

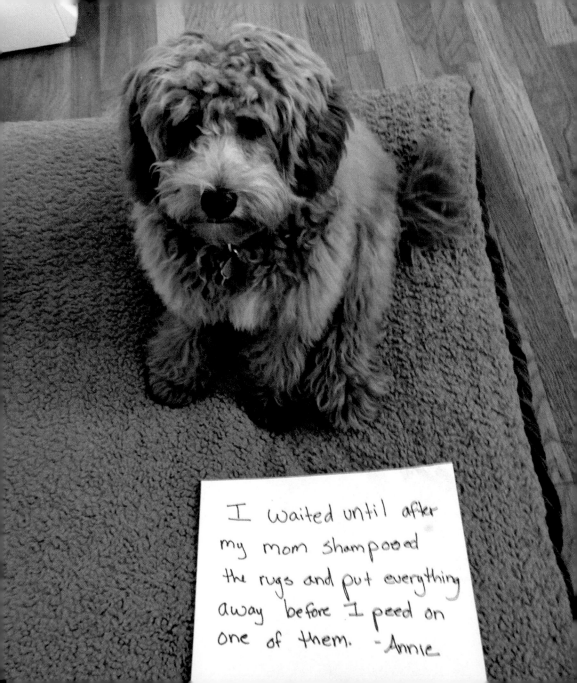

I waited until after my mom shampooed the rugs and put everything away before I peed on one of them. -Annie

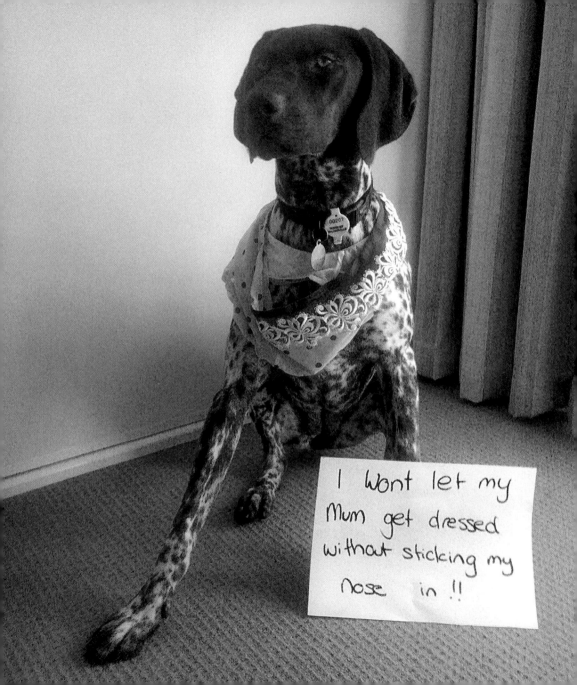

I wont let my Mum get dressed without sticking my nose in !!

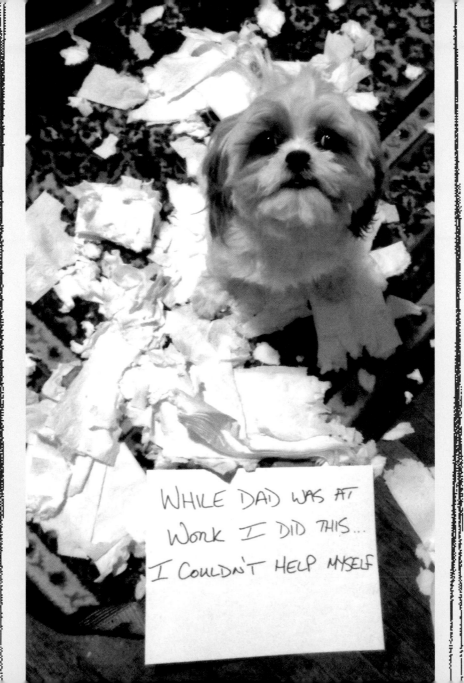

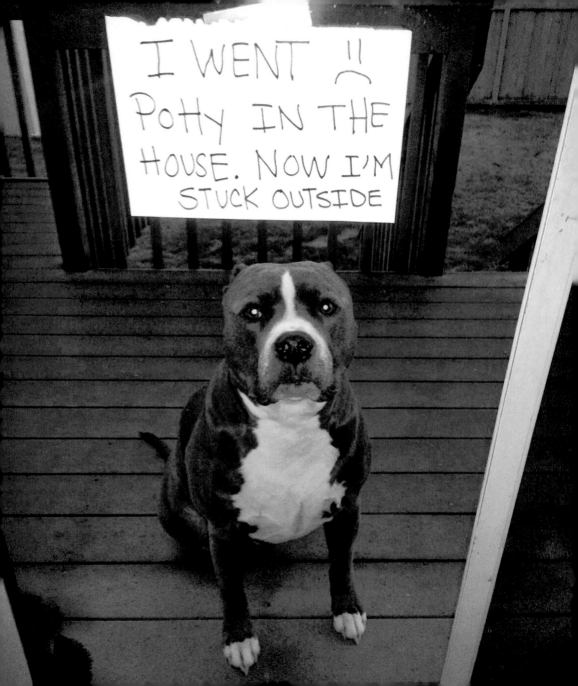

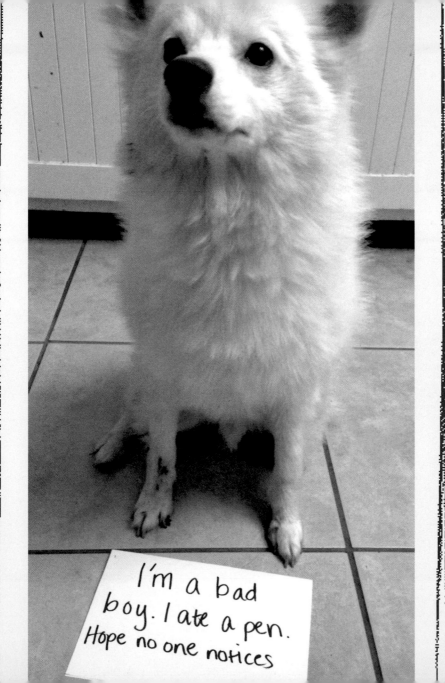

167

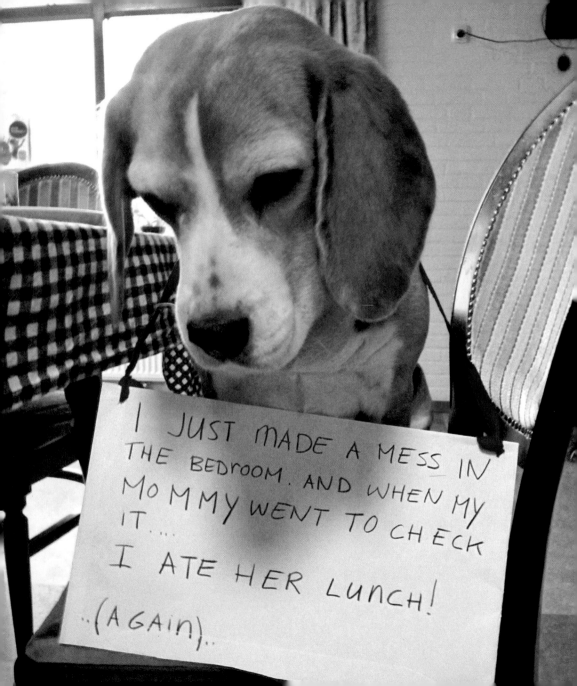

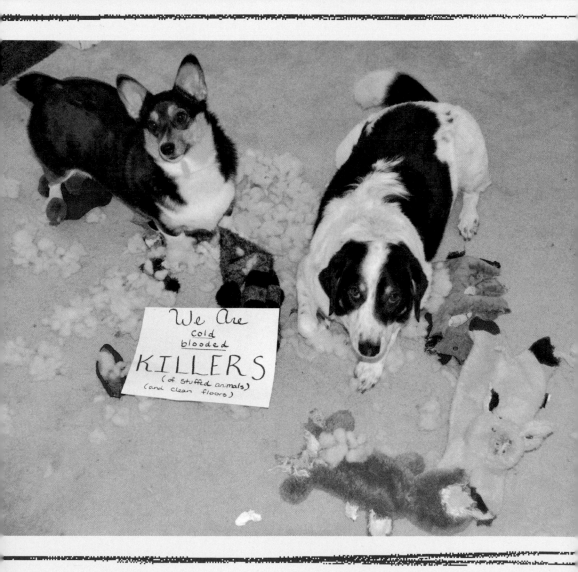

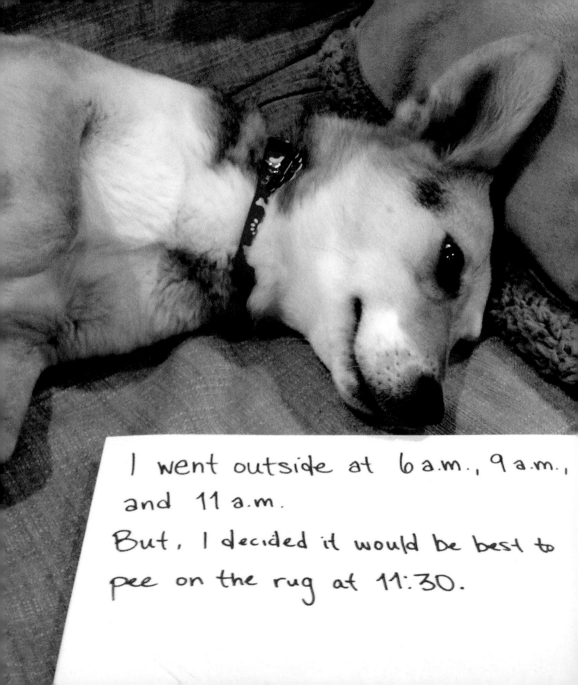

I went outside at 6 a.m., 9 a.m., and 11 a.m.
But, I decided it would be best to pee on the rug at 11:30.

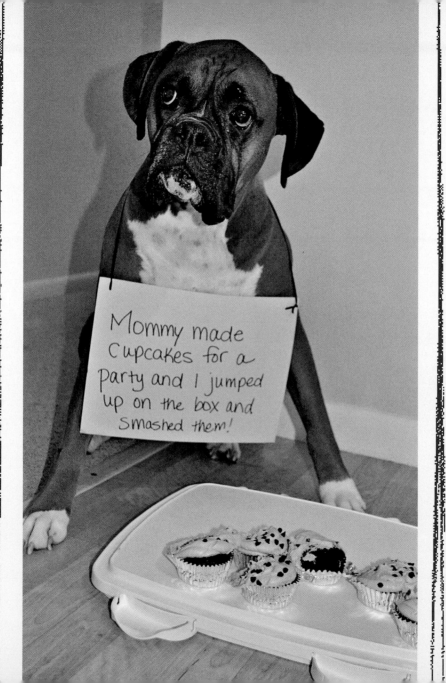

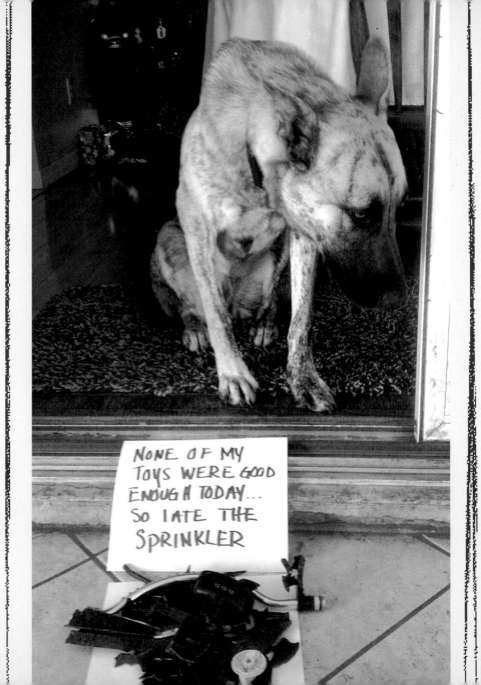

I style my little
brother's hair with
my drool

- Sugar

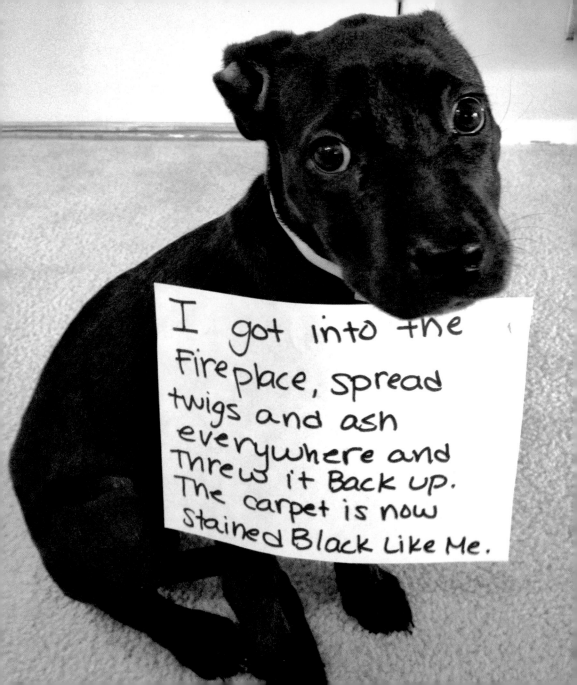

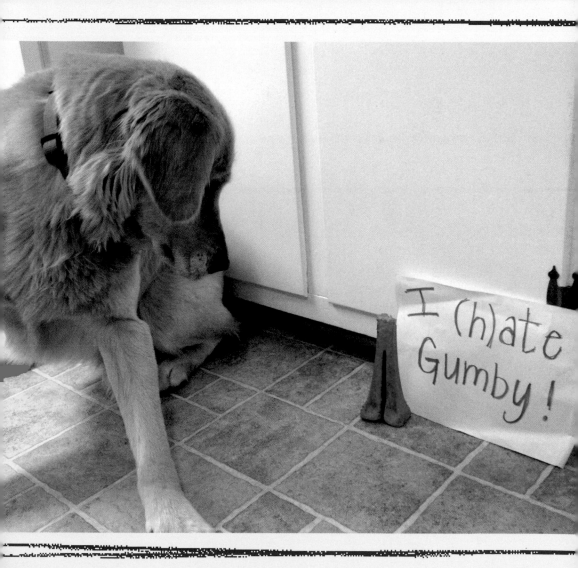

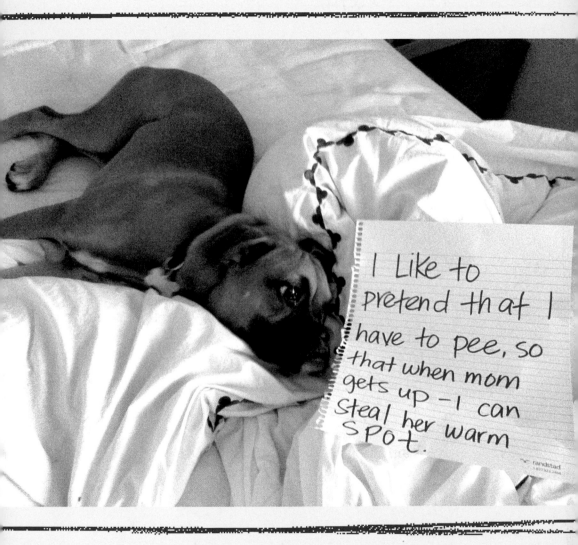

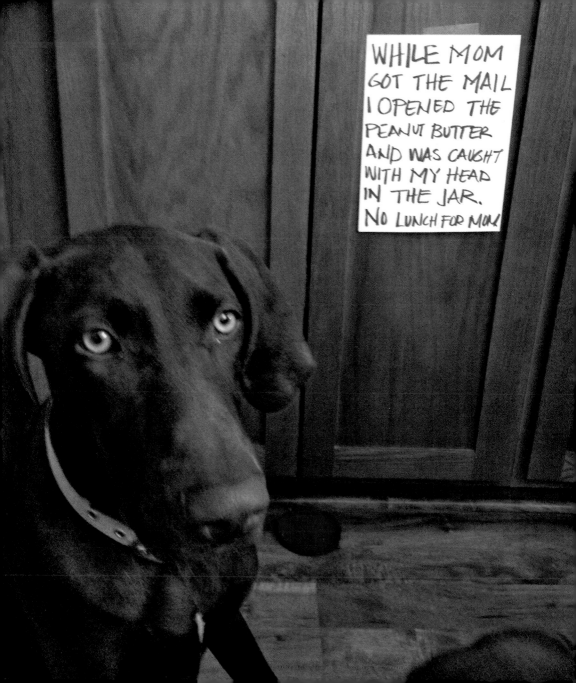

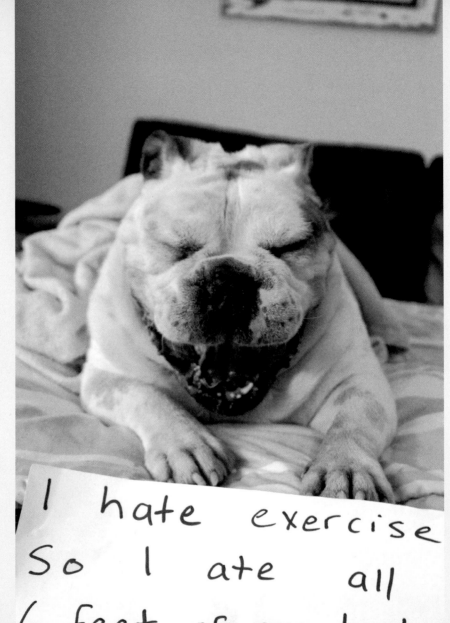

I hate exercise so I ate all 6 feet of my leash.

I eat garbage and then let my rotten, room-clearing gas seep out while I sleep SOUNDLY!!

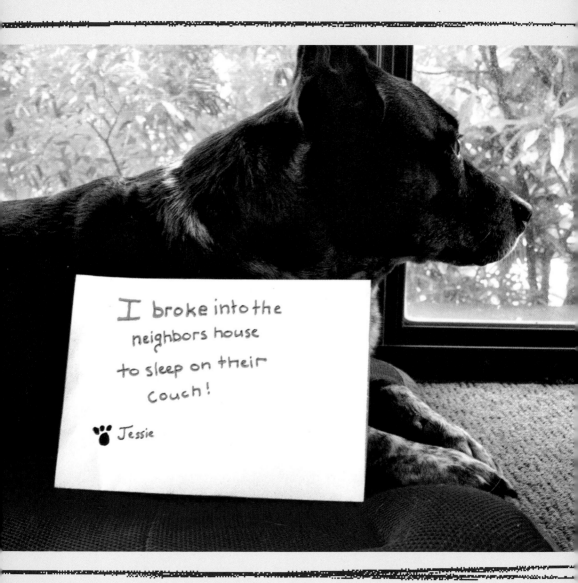

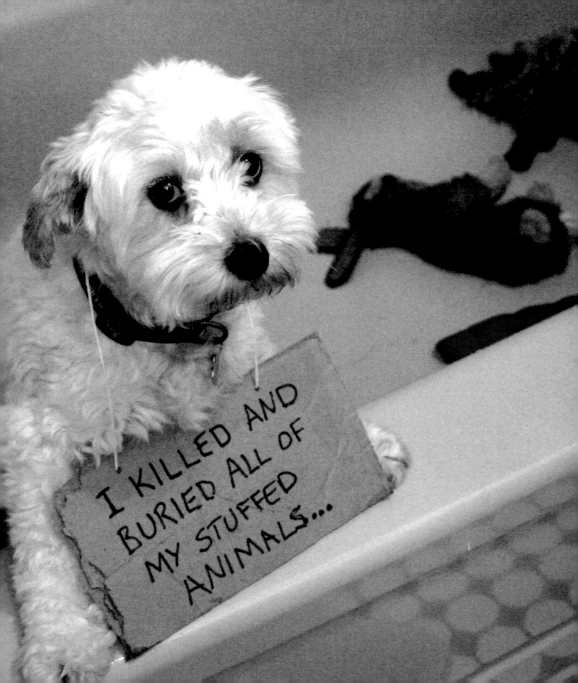

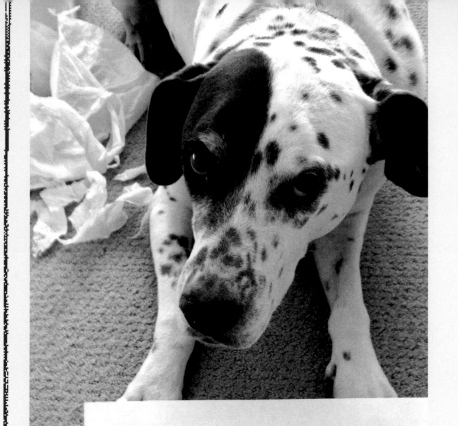

I waited for my parents to leave the house, then attacked the trash...

AGAIN

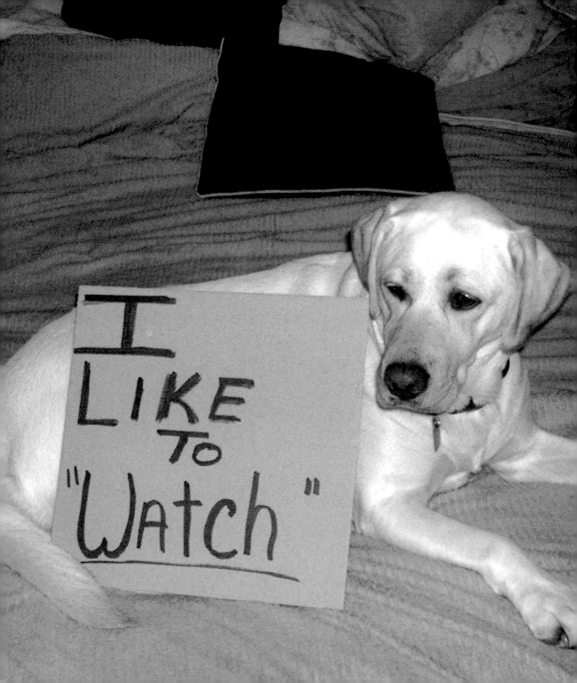

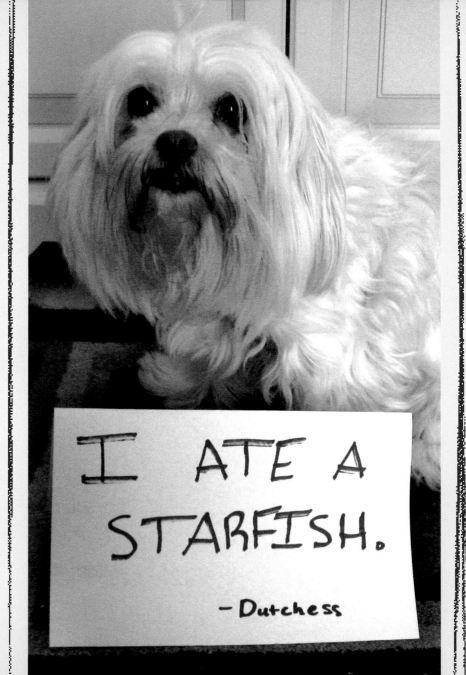

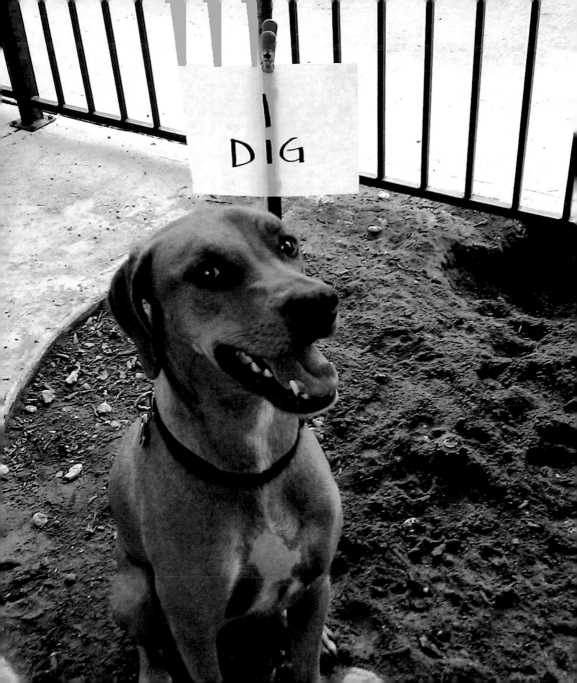

I am addicted
to hand lotion

(I am also afraid
of the camera.)

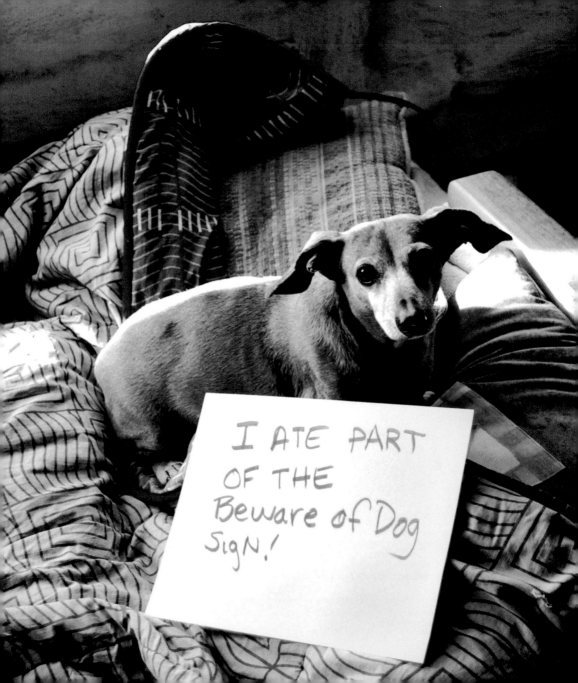

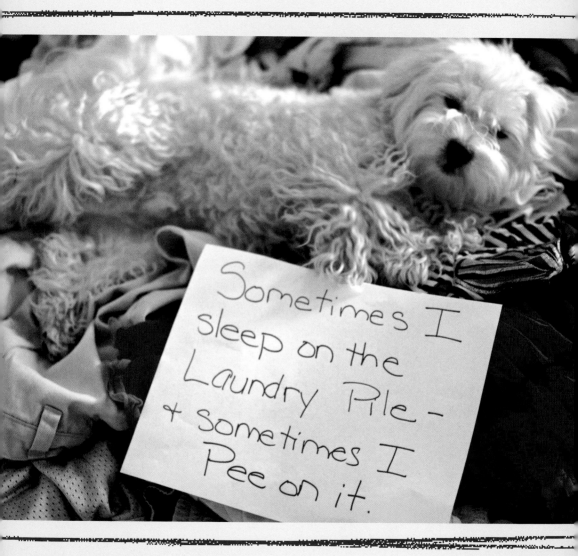

arg

YUM

The

tear

hew

FRIENDS

uilty

Love

Acknowledgments

I would like to take a moment to thank a few special people. Without them, this book would never have come to fruition. I'd like to thank my parents, Claude and Sylvia. Their unwavering love and encouragement has made me who I am today. My little brother, Alex: the barometer of what is hip or totally uncool (I definitely fit into the former category, for the first time). My best friend, Megan. She's there whether you're high or low (usually with wine). Everyone needs a Megan. Heather, my Californian ray of sunshine. My entire Tumblr community, who shared in my amazement and joy when I made it big. I'd like to thank Jairus of www.jairus.ca for being the best Web designer and developer. I'd also like to thank my agent, Kristyn Keene, over at ICM, for believing in me and being an all-around fantastic lady. Last, I'd like to thank Amanda Patten and her team at Three Rivers Press. Her continued enthusiasm and professionalism with a side of girlfriend made this process the most enjoyable and fulfilling months of my life.

Photo Credits

Page 11: Travis and Janet Boldt; page 12: Spanky the Mastiff, by Julie Wu; page 13: the Cipoletti family; page 14: Jacqueline Lusby; page 15: Michelle Shampine Smith; page 16: Celeste Aubin; page 17: Littleman, Ladybird, by Jaimie Trepanier; page 18: Lyndsay Chapman; page 19: Olivia, New York, NY; page 20: Catherine Hunsinger; page 21: Otis the Corgi at frogman.me, by Benjamin Grelle; page 22: photo by Sarah Fiske, www.sarahfiskephoto.com; page 23: Jennifer Anderson; page 24: Luci the former shelter dog, by Mona Langer; page 25: Penny the Dachshund, by Brandi Bolin; page 26: Andrea Taylor; page 27: Brad Newland; page 28: Skybo, by Summer Haines; page 29: Viky's little Dali, by Viky Durette; page 30: Trixie, by Jodi Thornton; page 31: Joan Cowburn; page 32: Daniel D. Hash; page 33: Sam, Whitney, and Lollie Kimball; page 34: Sara H.; page 35: Amanda Flourie vanHorn; page 36: Bingo and Martini, by Danae Andrie; page 37: Elyse and Marc Falco; page 38: Ranger Danger, by Kt Schramm and Hannah Robertson-Smith; page 39: K. A. Hayden; page 40: Sergeant Pepper First Christmas, photo taken by Samantha Weaver and Kyle Roberts; page 41: Lady the cereal killer, by Anita Taepke; page 42: Suzette LeClerc; page 43: Melinda Phillips; page 44: David Vanden Heuvel; page 45: skylarlechien.tumblr.com, by Bailey Kennedy; page 46: Sharon Riddick; page 47: Anthony Gabbianelli and Gipper; page 48: Patrice Bradley, Duluth, MN; page 49: Cheryl Dioguardi; page 50: Jennie Golick; page 51: Callie, by Lisa Hall; page 52: Mary Shields; page 53: Kristen Nichols; page 54: Allison M. Carlson; page 55: Wrigley, by Katie Doran-Patten; page 56: Alisia and Jeff Roos; page 57: Vincenzo Callari; page 58: Frederick the Bullheaded bulldog, by Alicia Dionne; page 59: Lisa and Billy Corbett; page 60: Tracie LeSar; page 61: David Parker; page 62: Kelly Ford; page 63: Andrew and Gabrielle K; page 64: Lauren Vitti; page 65: Michelle LaFrance; page 66: Ashley O'Leary; page 67: Irene Durbak; page 68: Ashley O'Brien; page 69: Elizabeth Bitler; page 70: photo by Lloyd and Susan Lambert; page 71: Picture of Ginger, by Ashton Harling and Jeff Pillsbury; page 72: Spoon, by Amy Small; page 73: Beth Bryant; page 74: Ginger M. Creel; page 75: Tracy McGoogan; page 76: Jennifer Lasky Russell; page 77: Deb Dulin; page 78: Krissy Helberg; page 79: Kyle and Heather Allison; page 80: Cassy Smith; page 81: Bridget Cleary; page 82: Vicky Kujawa; page 83: Kaitlin Johnson; page 84: Shelley Stancil; page 85: Rebekah Clinton; page 86: Vatche Kaprielian; page 87: Brent and Carmen Seib; page 88: Pumpkin the puggle, by Sierra K. Johnson; page 89: Nicole Mountain; page 90: Linus, by Bean Parker; page 91: Deborah Hart; page 92: Taylor L. Souder; page 93: Patty Gongaware; page 94: Lindsey Spinney; page 95: Maymo the lemon beagle, by Jeremy Lakaszcyck; page 96: the hole-digging Newfoundland Duchess, by JT and Brittany Wright; page 97: Kylie Della; page 98: Sharon Chee; page 99: Callie, by Gina Warburton; page 100: Jacqueline Lusby; page 101: Jenya Lemeshow; page 102: Lara Simmons; page 103: Andrea Shteynberg; page 104: Ahzi, by Bonnie Brett; page 105: Jennifer Miller; page 106: Sarah Doble; page 107: our lovable little handful, Maggie, by Mathew and Emily Haskins; page 108: Roxie, by Jaimie and Andrew Kane; page 109: AC Waller; page 110: Matthew Hockman; page 111: Elizabeth Brandstadt; page 112: Ariana and Catalina, by Ariana Trease; page 113: Hazel the retriever, by Barbara Malis; page 114: Jessie Frazier; page 115: Harriet, by Erin Manning; page 116: Gregory and Jennifer Weiler; page 117: Jennifer Bement; page 118: Megan McGaffigan; page 119: Amanda Watson; page 120: Gizma, by Stephanie Rudy; page 121: Caden the Caveman, by Rebecca Stewart; page 122: Marie Ramage; page 123: Hannah, by Heather Sorensen; page 124: Cookie, submitted by www.yvonneparks.com; page 125: D. Marty Fontaine; page 126: Heather Boczkiewicz; page 127: Nancy Spiewak; page 128: Gracie, by Melissa McGovern; page 129: Mary Linel; page 130: photo by Savanna D. Maue; page 131: Matthew and Kirsten McDaniel; page 132: Bradley Pepper; page 133: S.T. Ingram; page 134: Ashley Felger; page 135: Chris and Jenna Hough; page 136: Lauren Cash; page 137: Sally King; page 138: Charles Kaney; page 139: Peggy Casper; page 140: Amanda L. Miller; page 141: image courtesy of Stacie Erdman; page 142: Foxy the corgi and her people, by Rhiannon Riley; page 143: Doug, by Samantha and Steven Hampl; page 144: Ned Ryerson Bing!, by Jenny Rose Ryan; page 145: Caroline and Stephanie Novas; page 146: Jennifer Napolitano; page 147: Fiona Buchan; page 148: Matt Bogen; page 149: Becky McClary; page 150: Jessica Vaughan; page 151: Stephanie Salmon; page 152: Sarah Stafford; page 153: Ditka, our lovable bulldog, by Tim, Christy, Reagan, Lincoln, and McKinley Lowry; page 154: Julie Kriss; page 155: Lauren Jaglowski; page 156: Nina Denlew; page 157: Anna Langstaff; page 158: Jassmine Wood; page 159: Tillie and Shaun Mabbutt; page 160: Kassandra Semrau and Cheryl Schuerman; page 161: Sophie, Rob, and Hugo; page 162: Amy Johnson; page 163: Christine Kromer Park; page 164: Sarah Buck; page 165: "Bailey," photo by Mark Carter; page 166: Patricia Shelley; page 167: Andrew and Crystal Khan; page 168: Geertje Grom; page 169: Kathryn Kelly; page 170: Patrick O'Gara; page 171: Danielle Ran; page 172: Melissa Conley and Barbara S. Grassman; page 173: Jordan Curtis-Sherrod (Sugar's mom); page 174: Lew and Lisa Smith; page 175: Bear the Rescue Golden Lab, by Eileen and Josh Nelson; page 176: Patricia Año; page 177: Heather Chapa; page 178: Frank the tank, by Kaylan Massie; page 179: Ryder, by Kelly Brisson; page 180: Kara Crosser; page 181: Chelsea Caldwell and Kris Morness; page 182: Denise Klinger; page 183: Delores, by Lisa Boudreau; page 184: Nicole Tropea; page 185: Randy, by Laura and Tyler Gunn; page 186: Willow Scott; page 187: N. Bennett; page 188: Steve the maltese, by Celeta Bettison.